CW00683938

FROM SALON TO CELEBRITY

I dedicate this book to Maxine, my beautiful wife, friend, lover and guide.

FROM SALON TO CELEBRITY

the british hairdressing story

by Harold Leighton

seven
publications

Back cover : Barry Lategan

© 2004 Seven Publications
3, Square Moncey, 75009 Paris, France
T. +33 1 48 74 10 17
info@sevenpublications
www.tribu-te.com

© for the hairdressers photos: Harold Leighton
Texts : Marged Maggie Richards, London
Design: Mathias Dautriat, Paris

Printed in Italy
ISBN 2-9521628-0-8

Some of the photos in this book were impossible to trace and attribute.
My apologies to their authors, and thank you on behalf of those celebrated here.

How much does a hairstyle matter? Well, the truth is that hair speaks volumes. It is omnipresent. It is essential to our image of ourselves and the image we present to others. Hair tells a story, our own and other people's. It differentiates and distinguishes. It is loaded with powerful, sexual, political and socio-logical messages.

Historically a barometer of change, hair and the styling of it was only a concern of royalty and the upper classes, and the stylist involved was in the most part anonymous. All this changed radically in the 20th cen-tury, and even more dramatically in the 1950s and 1960s along with the cultural explosion in the worlds of art, architecture, music, film and fashion.

Britain emerged from the 1950s a changed country where the young took command. London became the youth culture's international capital, and along with the photographers, popstars, writers, interior designers, models and actors who became the new elite, so came pioneering hairdressers. By giving British men and women a new, modern aesthetic, these ground-breaking hairdressers literally made waves across the world. Think of Vidal Sassoon's geometric haircut worn by Mary Quant, Grace Coddington and Emmanuelle Khanh - or consider the Beatles' fringes and Twiggy's feathered crop crea-ted by Leonard and you get the picture.

Apart from ensuring that modern British women could "wash and go" with their new modern cuts and easier drying and styling techniques, talented British hairdressers (and that includes colourists) were also making headlines for themselves dating celebrities, travelling across the world and back to work on photographic shoots and fashion shows, not to mention advertising and promotion campaigns. TV docu-mentaries and Hollywood movies soon revolved around hair and the hairdresser's celebrity lifestyle. Then came *Hair,* the Broadway musical, and *Hairspray,* the movie. All this has only served to improve the indus-try's image and value and to turn the salon hairdresser into a celebrity. And then came the products.

Today, most hair products sold in salons, department stores, supermarkets and drug stores carry the name of a British hairdresser. As we know, these hairdressers have become household names fuelling what is now a multi-billion pound industry.

The UK has a stellar hair industry with some of the best talent in the world. During my seven years as beauty director on Vogue, and before that as the beauty director of Tatler, I have been lucky enough to work with many of the 72 exceptional stylists in this book. Master hairdressers are modern craftsmen who can liberate and transform with just a flick of their fingers and a snip of their scissors. Harold Leighton's book rightly celebrates them all.

KATHY PHILLIPS 2003

In 1998 I set out to write and photograph a book about those who had most influenced my life. In my time I have photographed such famous people as Pablo Picasso and President Ford. I have also been in the habit of photographing my friends, most of them hairdressers, who were or are famous in their own right. You must write a book about the industry, said my wife Maxine. What a great idea I thought, and almost five years later here we are.

My career in hairdressing started in 1947 as a young teenager in a salon in Harrow where a kindly relative (my uncle Alf) took me under his wing. I stayed for one year, leaving at Christmas 1947 for Romaine's of Park West on the Edgware Road, where the owners Albert Simmons and Leonard Stein taught me the rudiments of hairdressing and much about life, aided, I recall, by a small band of ladies who showed me the art of cleaning towels and toilets, sweeping floors, and removing the hair from trolley wheels.

The years that followed saw a remarkable flowering of creativity at Romaine's. Soon to join the salon was another young group; Leslie Green, Connie Baker, Gerard Saper and others who quickly became friends, rising stars and later household names. One of the most famous of this group was Vidal Sassoon, then unknown. The sheer enthusiasm and camaraderie of our team has had a lasting effect on my life for which I am forever grateful.

Inevitably, the group dispersed. I left to join Dumas and on to build two salons with Gerard Saper in Harrow and Wembley. Five years later, with Maxine, I daringly opened the first salon and fashion boutique in Hampstead. We took another large leap into the unknown by taking on board Caroline Neville to organise our public relations. She achieved astonishing publicity for us both, and later built herself a worldwide reputation as the MD of Caroline Neville Associates, now Neville McCarthy Associates. Her help with this book has been invaluable.

These were exciting days. Swinging London and the 60s; Beatlemania at its height: invitations to film premieres; celebrity friends. Invitations to the USA through Marlo Thomas gave us the opportunity to meet Jack Kennedy, Judy Garland, Lauren Bacall, Lucille Ball, Rock Hudson, Julie Christie, Dusty Springfield, the Rolling Stones… Name them, Maxine dressed them, and I styled their hair.

Soon I was working for the best-selling glossy magazines; with the most popular models from Jean Shrimpton to Kate Moss, and also with major photographers of the ilk of Terence Donovan, Cecil Beaton and Helmut Newton. I created exaggerated looks for the biggest cosmetic brands of the day such as Revlon and Max Factor. And when not creating for their campaigns I was travelling the world presenting the best of British hair fashion for Wella, Schwartzkopf, L'Oreal and Redken. But times move on, the Hampstead days were over and I opened the Dorothy Gray salon on Conduit Street, today the home of Daniel Hersheson. I later spent 18 happy years as creative consultant for both Essenelle and Glemby, two of the largest salon owners in the world which were later bought by the Regis.

And then in 1984 my dear friend Paul Mitchell asked me to represent his new line of hair products in Europe. My initial response was: "I am a hairdresser, I do not want to be a shampoo salesman." But Maxine loved the products that Paul kept sending us from Hawaii to our cottage in Mill Hill. As usual, she was right and I was wrong. Little did I know the bottles contained a magic formula that would be my next professional passion.

My photographer's instinct was inspired by such master photographers as Barry Lategan, David Bailey, Norman Eales and Clive Arrowsmith. I thank them, and acknowledge the debt I owe them.

I am a very lucky man to have this opportunity to turn my hobby into a book. I love this industry!

My thanks goes out to all the icons for the trust and confidence they have shown in me over the last four years of nagging emails, letters and phone calls. They all came up trumps. I was, on many occasions, very nervous because they'd worked with the world's top photographers. Some, such as Anthony Mascolo, Desmond Murray, Stephen Way and Robert Lobetta, have themselves turned into snappers, so to me it was like performing to an audience of superstars. Many of the newer names didn't know me as a crimper because I've been out of the limelight for so long. But they were all kindness itself, and for that I humbly thank them.

I'd especially like to thank the gracious Ann Herman, event coordinator of the Fellowship for British Hairdressing, for introducing me to Bertrand Fontaine, managing director of L'Oreal Professional Products in the UK. You have to admire the man's taste in photography. As he closed my portfolio, he looked at me and said: "I like your work. I like the story. Can you just make one simple change and go for British instead of world icons?" Easy, as the Brits really did start the hairdressing revolution in the 1960s.

With the help of Stephen Mesiass, Anne also allowed me the privilege of having three photoshoots with the Fellowship - two at Hyde Park and one on the magical night of the 31st August 2003 when dear Anne was knighted at the Royal Lancaster Hotel. Such a large group of leading hairdressers posing together has never happened before. We were making history.

Bertrand led me to publisher Mike Vincent of Seven Publications in Paris. On phoning Mike, he was ready to jump on a plane from Paris within days to help me plan the process. Jason Kearns in Toronto put me in touch with Helen Oppenheim, and lo and behold, in a blink I received an email listing all the American contact details I'd asked for.

Travel, film, processing, enlargements - creating a portfolio is a costly pastime; one I probably wouldn't have been able to indulge in were it not for the swift sponsorship generously given to me by Paul Finkelstein, CEO of Regis International. Thank you so much for your support, Paul. My personal thanks to all the PRs, PAs, partners and Upfront TV/Celebrities Worldwide, without whom we'd still be waiting for biographies...

Thank you to Rosalie Bessone for Teasie Weasie's story; Lisa Shepherd and Claire Shread for their help in compiling Umberto Giannini's pages; and Michele Warshaw and Nicky French for sharing their father's stories.

Caroline Neville is chairman of Neville McCarthy Associates, one of the most prestigious PR companies in the UK. She became my and Maxine's PR in the 1960s, and we've been friends ever since. It was Caroline who launched my first two books: *Haircutting for Everyone* and *The Complete Book of Haircare*, which sold over a quarter of a million copies. I thank her from the bottom of my heart for putting so much energy and effort into taking me on again.

Upon hearing about my latest project, she introduced me to freelance journalist Marged Richards, who came on board as my ghostwriter. My hat goes off to this dynamic young lady who's shown so much determination and perseverance in helping me complete this mammoth task.

Finally, thanks to Joycellyn Akuffo for her proofreading skills, and gifted designer Mathias Dautriat for patiently making this such a visually exciting book.

HAROLD LEIGHTON

I met Harold Leighton 54 years ago as an apprentice at Romaine's on Edgware Road, near Marble Arch in London. An extraordinary team of young aspiring crimpers, our leader was Leslie Green, who'd returned from the army in 1945. With his wife Connie, Leslie, Harold, the self-assured Gerard London and myself created an exuberant working ambience. Although we lived and breathed hairdressing, we hadn't thought about changing things then.

Independently, Harold, Gerard and I found ourselves applying our craft at Dumas in holy Mayfair. Frank Blashke, a top international competition winner, was there to motivate us, as was Sylvio Camillo. And then there was Raymond, who made us believe in the heights we could reach.

Naturally, we went our separate ways. Harold created a niche for himself as a superb hair artist and a walking encyclopedia of hair. What he doesn't know, his dynamic, vivacious wife Maxine will. His partner in many exploits, choosing Maxine confirmed Harold's eye for aesthetics.

The desire to create this book exemplifies his total immersion in, and commitment to the betterment of, our craft. It is the same energy that propelled him deep into the night, putting shows together and coming up with new products. His multifaceted talent has inspired us all.

There's only one Harold Leighton. I don't think the industry could handle two!

VIDAL SASSOON, 2004

For over half a century a group of men and women have worked in many different ways to change the world of hairdressing. The way hair is cut, styled, coloured and dressed has been transformed. But, more importantly, the world's perception of hairdressers has changed. Where once it was considered a job, hairdressing is now a highly respected profession. It is a career path that attracts a certain character who is dedicated, ambitious, keen to enjoy recognition, but also generous enough to unreservedly share knowledge and skills in a way not encountered within other professions.

Raymond (Teasie Weasie) 1911 -1992, can be credited with being the catalyst for this change. In the austerity of post war Britain, we needed glamour and pzazz. Raymond held court to London's society in his flamboyant, baroque inspired salon in Mayfair. Champagne flowed from fountains, caviar was served on silver spoons and, whilst, his clients hair was teased and lacquered into wondrous shapes, their poodles were coloured pink to match their latest Parisian outfits. Raymond was feted all round the world; he dressed the hair of Kings and Queens, the aristocracy and Hollywood film stars. He discovered the art of public relations and brought hairdressing into the public arena. He was the first hairdresser to have his own television show, the first to have his own product line, the first to make front page news when his horse Rag Trade won the National. He was, in fact, our first celebrity hairdresser.

Since the heady 1950s, each decade has spawned its own hair heroes and each can be likened to a small acorn from which hair artistry has developed and grown. In the 60s, Vidal Sassoon invented the cut and blow-dry when, inspired by the way Mary Quant cut fabric, Sassoon applied the same technique to hair. A mere mile away in Mayfair Leonard applied this technique to an unknown Neasden model, the picture, published in Vogue, led to the 60s fashion revolution and invented the original supermodel, Twiggy.

Meanwhile the original colour guru, Daniel Galvin, used primary colours for the first time. Technicolor hair, when unleashed on an unsuspecting Kings Road, made punk rockers a tourist attraction for London.

In the 70s Heinz Schumi invented his Schumi Shapers which were set to create a million curls and I created the Scrunch which changed the way women dried their hair. During the 80s, Simon Forbes, the alternative hairdresser of the time, came up with Monofibre extensions, a brilliant idea for weird and wacky hair that has now entered the mainstream.

Empire building started in the mid 80s when the Mascolo brothers harnessed their artistic and business skills to develop Toni & Guy. The 90s saw a new breed of stylist - determined, hungry to succeed, both artistically and professionally. Whilst the likes of Eugene Souleiman and Guido set the trends on the international catwalks; young rebels like Antoinette Beenders and Lee Stafford took their inspiration from past masters but did it their way. We have always had our showmen like Robert Croemans on stage and Robert Lobetta in print, but as we turn into the new millennium there is yet another a new generation - young men like Angelo Seminara, who have begun to hit the headlines with their particular take on hair.

This photographic book is a unique collection of imagery that aims to bring together the diverse artistry and characters of the people who have influenced hairdressing over the past 50 years. The book is Harold Leighton's baby. For the past four years he has lived and breathed Hairdressing Icons.? He has nagged, cajoled and sometimes begged people to take part; to help him put down on paper a history of this century's most influential hairdressers. The book is intended to chronicle our hair heroes but each picture aims to capture a part of their personality, perhaps unknown to others. For Harold it has been a mission. For all who read and enjoy, I hope it will be an inspiration.

TREVOR SORBIE

Harold Leighton has always been a great icon in the hairdressing industry. I remember seeing his stand at Salon International in the late 1970s; he had created a larger-than-life size model of himself with a moving mouth that spoke to the audience. It was an effective idea that certainly caused a stir and left a lasting impression. Hairdressing has always been his love and his styles have inspired many.

Harold is an innovator; he transformed the technique of blow-drying when he designed and produced his own line of brushes. As a hairdresser, he knew exactly what was required for an effective hairdressing tool.

Harold's transition from hairdressing to photography through his PR experience has been a natural progression for him. He approaches photography with immense enthusiasm, bringing out the best in his subjects.

I know that this book will be a huge success as it is a unique concept that portrays his love and support for the industry. I wish him all the success he deserves.

ANTHONY MASCOLO

Hairdresser - the word conveys an attention to grooming that even our primate ancestors were preoccupied with. Today, our appearance is dependent on the skill and understanding of the practitioners of the craft.

The history of crimpers in Britain carries many great names, amongst them Raymond "Teasie Weasie" - a phrase he used on television to describe the delicate arrangement of a piece of hair, and which became his nickname.

The roll-call of my time in the world of fashion photography led to collaborations with the pioneering Rose Evansky, Edward Morris of Andre Bernard, and most notably Vidal Sassoon, from whose salons emerged great followers such as Leonard Lewis whose haircut of a 16-year-old schoolgirl photographed by me launched Twiggy. Leonard's salon in turn produced Nicky Clarke and John Frieda.

Within this labyrinth of example and influence, Harold Leighton fluttered his nimble fingers in Hampstead and Harrods. I applaud his enthusiasm and ability as hairdresser, photographer and PR, and proffer my tribute to him.

BARRY LATEGAN

THE ICONS

Photo: Barry Cook

In his present post as technical artistic director he is responsible for the standard and curriculum at Aveda's Advanced Academies, and for the biannual seasonal collections (cut, colour and make-up). Working closely with Aveda's research department David helps develop the brand's colour line, and more generally, the company's image throughout the industry. "My job is to connect us closer to fashion," he says.

"I can colour hair for a photoshoot, advertising campaign, fashion show, hair show, television series, a play or film - there aren't many jobs that offer such a variety of enjoyment," enthuses David. His advice to aspiring crimpers is to work with experienced hairdressers at every opportunity. "When young you have boundless energy and enthusiasm - don't think about money, think about learning as much you can. Money comes with age, experience and knowledge," he adds.

David, like many featured in this book, has now made his home in America, although his education commitments keep him on regular flights abroad. He is an example of how the Brits can succeed in the US, where talent is appreciated and used to the full, and where our small British band is steadily making its mark.

Hairdressing is similar to the fashion industry, where designer collections are copied and adapted to the high street. A parallel process happens when our best British hairdressers travel the world creating trendsetting ideas that end-up in local salons.

Everything about the industry excites David: "There is so much to learn, especially in colour where technology is constantly evolving. Salons are at last realising the full potential of employing technical specialists, and clients are often more loyal to their colourist than to their stylist. Colour is the fastest growing sector of the industry, generating millions of pounds worldwide." Now that is exciting.

WORLD-CLASS COLOURIST, DAVID ADAMS HAS EARNED INDUSTRY-WIDE RESPECT THROUGH HIS SKILL AS AN EDUCATOR, AND HIS ABILITY TO RECOGNISE AND INSPIRE CREATIVE TALENT. IN EARLY 2004, HE BECAME THE FIRST COLOURIST TO HEADLINE THE AUSTRALIAN HAIR CONGRESS SHOW.

I KNOW DAVID THROUGH HIS COLOURING SEMINARS WITH DANIEL GALVIN, ANNIE HUMPHRIES AND TREVOR SORBIE, WHO IN HIS EARLY DAYS NURTURED HIS TALENT AND TAUGHT HIM THE SKILLS HE IS NOW PASSING ON TO THE AVEDA TRIBE AROUND THE WORLD.

2003: Technical Artistic Director of Aveda
2002: HaircolorUSA Most Inspirational Education Award
2001: Technical Director of new Aveda Institute Covent
       Garden, London
       Hair Color USA Most Innovative Technique Award
       Global Technical Director of Aveda
2000: Aveda Master of the Arts Award
1998: Opening of The London Academy for Hair Colour
       at the Aveda Institute
       Aveda 20/20 Vision Show, New York
       The Art of Hair Colouring by David Adams and
       Jacki Wadeson
1997: Technical Director, Aveda Concept salons
1993: Technical Director, Jo Hansford salon
1983: Colourist, Trevor Sorbie salon
1979: Colourist, Vidal Sassoon salon
1976: Colourist, Daniel Galvin salon

RESPONSIBLE FOR THE TRAINING OF MANY OF TODAY'S TOP HAIRDRESSERS, TONY HAS BEEN IN THE BUSINESS FOR MORE THAN 40 YEARS. HE BEGAN HIS CAREER IN 1960 AS A SASSOON APPRENTICE, AND WITHIN A YEAR WAS APPOINTED VIDAL'S PERSONAL ASSISTANT.

Photo: Tony Beckermann

2002: Founds TSB-cutting edge resources
Vice President of Creative and Artistic Development,
The Haircolorxperts
1999: Matrix Essentials C.R.A.F.T. Cutting Innovation Award
1998: Abbie Award for directing the best music score for a video
1995: Hosted Vidal Sassoon 50th Anniversary
1995: Member of the Society of Cosmetic Chemists
1994: World Master Award
Named one of the Vidal Sassoon original "Famous 20"
1993: Who's Who
1990-1994: Stage Artist of the Year
1975: Opened first Vidal Sassoon advanced haircutting academy in the USA
1961 -1963: Vidal Sassoon's personal assistant
1960: Apprentice to Vidal Sassoon

I know Tony from the Trevor Sorbie and Roger Thompson days, when I used to go to my friend's salon and *varda* - the Vidal word for 'to watch and learn'. In a few years, like Paul, Lobetta, the Chadwicks, the Doves and oh so many Brits, he left for the States. And made it. As director of training at the Madison Avenue salon, where he introduced and taught geometric precision cutting to American and Canadian hairdressers and barbers. In those days US hairdressing was nothing to write home about, apart from a few exceptions such as Ara Gallant, Kenneth Battel and Sydney Guileroff. Tony also helped open the first Vidal Sassoon advanced haircutting academy in the country, in San Francisco.

After 16 years with Sassoon, Tony co-formed Fashion Media Inc., dedicated to educating hairdressers. There he co-produced the first consumer Hair Fair for the beauty industry.

In 1995, he joined Matrix Essentials to help develop new concepts in haircare, colour and chemical service products, and coach the famous Matrix Design Team. His list of contributions to the company's top-selling innovations, products and services includes the C.R.A.F.T cutting system, which led to C.R.A.F.T. Color and C.R.A.F.T Texture.

In 2002, Tony created a strategic alliance with franchise company HCX, the haircolorxperts, and was appointed vice-president of creative and artistic development.

Today, he heads his own consulting company called TSB cutting-edge resources, specialising in creative product development, hair design, coaching, consulting and presentations. As an active member of the Society of Cosmetic Chemists, Tony works with some of the top scientists in the world.

LIVING ON THE RIVER THAMES IN THE HEART OF LONDON IS USUALLY A SIGN THAT YOU'VE MADE IT. THIS IS WHERE I FOUND ANTOINETTE BEENDERS' NEW ABODE, AND WHAT AN IMPRESSION IT MAKES - A TESTAMENT TO THE HARD WORK SHE'S PUT INTO HER GLITTERING CAREER.

Today global style director of Aveda and creative director of the Aveda Salon at London's Aveda Institute, she started her rise to the top as a 14-year-old Saturday girl in a salon in Haarlem, Holland, and within two years was working full-time as a stylist.

As a young 18-year-old manager, regularly attending British hairdressing seminars, she was attracted to work in London as a junior to Trevor Sorbie in his Covent Garden salon. Four years later, she became Trevor's art director and started winning the first of a long list of awards. The pair worked together for 12 years before Aveda approached Antoinette in 1998 to open their Harvey Nichols salon.

Antoinette is smart and creative. While attempting to create a modern version of the 70s Farah Fawcett hairstyle, she invented the Clippertwist, a technique performed on a length dry flat wrapped hair, which leaves a heavy-layered shape easily that can be easily blow-dried into a flicky look.

Winning Fellowship Hairdresser of the Year in 1999 was a major honour: "Feeling valued by my peers means a lot to me and you can only imagine when I won again in 2002 - the first member to do so twice since the Fellowship for British Hairdressing was founded. My feet still haven't touched the ground." However, she's keen to say that she still has unfulfilled ambition.

"I am fortunate to work with teams in America and the UK," says Antoinette. "All my team members are winners in their own right and could be part of the elite of tomorrow. Their talent, hard work and dedication is second to none."

The industry is welcoming more and more women who are challenging the guys to the top spots. Successes such as Beverly Cobella, Lisa Sheperd, Jo Hansford, Sacha Mascolo Tarbuck are showing aspiring girls that there is room at the top of the hairdressing ladder.

2002: Fellowship Hairdresser of the Year
2001: Masterjam Minneapolis
2000: Master of Arts Award
Session Hairdresser of the Year Finalist
Invented the Clippertwist technique
1999: Fellowship Hairdresser of the Year
Modern Salon Best 75 Educators of the
Millennium Nominee
1998: Invented the Backslash hair cut
Most Newsworthy Female Hair Designer
Worldwide
(IBS Award), New York
1997: London Hairdresser of the Year
1996: London Hairdresser of the Year
1995: Avant-Garde Hairdresser of the Year
London Hairdresser of the Year Nominee
1994: Appointed International Artistic Director for
Trevor Sorbie International
1992: Appointed UK Artistic Director for Trevor
Sorbie International
1990: Cosmopolitan Woman of the Year Finalist

SINCE LEAVING NEW ZEALAND FOR BRITAIN IN 1987, PATRICK CAMERON HAS BEEN INSPIRING HAIRDRESSERS WORLDWIDE WITH HIS THEATRICAL PRESENTATIONS, JUSTLY EARNING HIS PLACE IN HAIRDRESSING'S HALL OF FAME AS ONE OF THE WORLD'S MOST RESPECTED PLATFORM ARTISTS. "EDUCATION IS ITS OWN REWARD," HE SAYS.

One of the most charming and talented people you could meet, I've known Patrick and his abundance of curls for years. He specialises in long hair; the longer it is, the happier he is working on it. "If you approach long hairdressing simply and methodically, as you do when you learn to cut, the results will speak for themselves," he argues. Those acquainted with his step-by-step books and video series on dressing long hair would agree.

The world's most prestigious industry events are a second home to Patrick, who spends the majority of his time presenting at major shows such as Cosmoprof, The Congress, The Alternative Hair Show and Salon International. "I love performing and always try to combine education and entertainment," he explains. "I break down my techniques into simple steps so that the audience understands what I am trying to share with them. If I feel I'm losing their attention, I might do something impromptu like dance with my model, which usually does the trick."

At the Patrick Cameron School in London, students are offered the opportunity to work one-to-one with the craftsman. The way the school is set up allows Patrick to take it on the road, where he has so far trained hairdressers in Slovenia, Malta, Germany, Ireland, Singapore, Australia, New Zealand and America. "Whether I am doing shows for large audiences with Wella, or hosting an intimate workshop at the school, my message is the same: education is everything," he says. Perhaps not everything - known for style and elegance, he works closely with designer Marco Erbi each year to create a stunning collection of hair and fashion predictions.

Like most elite hairdressers, Patrick lives on aeroplanes (it wouldn't surprise me if our industry keeps BA in business), but far from exhausting him, he finds inspiration in his travels. "I'm intrigued by local traditions, influences which I fuse with street fashion, and a touch of haute couture to create classic long hair looks with a contemporary twist," he says.

JENNIFER CHEYNE STARTED OUT AGED 13 AS A SATURDAY GIRL. TODAY, SHE IS THE DRIVING FORCE BEHIND ONE OF SCOTLAND'S MOST SUCCESSFUL HAIRDRESSING COMPANIES, AND DIRECTOR 11 BUSINESSES, INCLUDING SIX SALONS, TWO HAIRDRESSING SCHOOLS AND AN INTERNATIONAL PRODUCT LINE.

HER BASIC TRAINING IN HAIRDRESSING AND BUSINESS MANAGEMENT WAS AT STEWARTS, WHICH IS ON EDINBURGH'S PRINCES STREET. AT 18, JENNIFER BECAME BRITAIN'S FIRST FEMALE BARBER AT HIS HAIR, THE FASHIONABLE SALON OF TWO OTHER SUCCESSFUL SCOTS, CHARLIE MILLER AND CHARLIE MEARNS. "I WOULD GO TO WORK AT 9AM IN MY MINI SKIRT AND TRENDY LITTLE MINI CAR," SHE RECALLS. "THE QUEUE TO ENTER THE SALON OFTEN WENT DOWN THE STAIRS AND ALONG THE ROAD."

After three years with His Hair, and a further four with Brian Drumm, the 23-year-old entrepreneur borrowed £2,000 from her father and set up the first Cheyne's salon. She repaid him in six months, opening new salons only when existing ones were 90% full and wouldn't lose out to the new site. Today, Jennifer's six Edinburgh city centre salons employ a loyal team of 160 - 50 of whom have been with the company for more than 15 years. Five senior managers have stayed for 20 years, and one of her salon directors has been with the company right from the beginning. Amongst those who have inspired Jennifer, she names Robert Lobetta, Charles Worthington, Alan Peters, John Frieda and Leslie Spears.

Since its launch in 1988, her hairdressing school Cheynes Education has taught over 250,000 students, and its foundation training programme trains thousands in salons every year. For a young person pursing a hairdressing career, getting a start at Cheynes is the equivalent of going to Oxford or Cambridge.

In 1998, Jennifer became the first female president of the Fellowship for British Hairdressing, a role she used to modernise the organisation and improve morale. "My aim was to put something back into the industry I love," she says. Two years later she became chancellor.

Voted one of the 100 most influential women in business by the Sunday Herald, and Scottish Hairdresser of the Year, her knowledge of both the artistic and commercial sides of our industry is considerable. She tirelessly works with major manufacturers developing and promoting products, teaches business seminars, and when she can, indulges in her favourite hobby - design. "I have lots of ideas and plans for the future and who knows what exciting opportunities will come my way. Here's to the next 27 years!" she enthuses.

To take her photograph, I met Jennifer and her husband Cliff on Miami's South Beach, where she'd stopped off especially, en route to Brazil. What a wonderful life the icons enjoy when the hard work pays off!

2000: Chancellor of the Fellowship for British Hairdressing
1998: President of the Fellowship for British Hairdressing
1997: World Masters of the Craft Award, New York
1996: Vice-President of the Fellowship for British Hairdressing
1995: Tribute to Excellence, Philadelphia International Hair and Beauty Festival
1989: Partner, Cheynes Training and Cheynes Education
1976: Chairman Cheynes Management

NICKY AND LESLEY SHARE AN ABUNDANCE OF TALENT FOR BOTH HAIRDRESSING AND MARKETING. WITH HIS FLOWING RED HAIR AND READY SMILE, NICKY HAS MADE A LASTING IMPRESSION ON THE BRITISH MEDIA AS "THE WORLD'S MOST NEWSWORTHY HAIRDRESSER."

IT FEELS LIKE ONLY YESTERDAY THAT I WAS AT THE OPENING PARTY OF THEIR BERKELEY SQUARE SALON, JOSTLING WITH HUNDREDS OF FACES WAITING TO CATCH A GLIMPSE OF ONE OF THE MOST FAMOUS OF ALL - THE DUCHESS OF YORK'S. OF COURSE THE NEXT DAY'S PAPERS WERE FULL OF THE PARTY. TYPICAL OF THE CLARKE'S - THEY'RE FOREVER HITTING THE HEADLINES.

2003: Hairomatherapy relaunched
2002: Second salon opens in Manchester
2001: Nicky Clarke Colour launched
2000: Colour Therapy launched
1996: Nicky Clarke Electric range launched
1993: Hairomatherapy launched
1991: Nicky Clarke salon opens in Mayfair

Managing director of the Nicky Clarke brand, Lesley, arrived on the hair scene in the late 80s through Nicky, an up-and-coming young hairdresser and international session stylist. From the outset, Nicky regarded Lesley as "first in command," and in 1990 she convinced him that the time was right to open their own salon. Its Mayfair doors opened the following May to an inexorable flow of celebrities and royalty. Nicky has dominated the hair world since, winning top awards including Session Hairdresser of the Year, London Hairdresser of the Year and British Hairdresser of the Year.

Lesley quickly recognised that Nicky's success should be consolidated by the launch of a signature haircare range. Her interest in aromatherapy and expertise in formulations, together with Nicky's hair expertise, led to the award-winning Hairomatherapy, and later Colour Therapy and Nicky Clarke Colour. Launched in 1996, sales of the signature Electric range were so high they marked Nicky Clarke out as Britain's fastest-growing electrical haircare product company.

Although Nicky is the inspiration behind the salons' creative success, it is Lesley's first-class business acumen, and formal experience of running her own label, that drive their empire forward. Unfortunately, in the mid 90s they ended their personal relationship, but continue to be inseparable business partners and best friends.

We next got together to take their picture. While Nick was preparing Lesley's gorgeous hair, I was planning the location. The all white lounge, with a white grand piano in the bay window of Nicky's home is so atmospheric that I turned to him and said: "I'd love to do a Baker Boys-style shot with Lesley on the top of the piano". Just then she came down the stairs dressed in the sexiest of evening gowns.

Once the shoot was over, the pair jumped in to a chauffeur-driven limo and were whisked to an awards ceremony at the Albert Hall. Surely, they won a trophy for Best Looking Couple in London?

BEVERLY AND ANESTIS OPENED THEIR FIRST SALON IN 1980 IN MAYFAIR, FOLLOWED BY A SECOND JUST TWO YEARS LATER. FAR FROM RESTING ON THEIR LAURELS, THE HUSBAND AND WIFE TEAM SET OFF TO TOUR THE WORLD TEACHING AND DEMONSTRATING TO ENTHUSIASTIC AUDIENCES SOME OF THE MOST CREATIVE AND EXCITING SHOWS IN THE INDUSTRY. THEY EVENTUALLY STOPPED-OFF IN NEW YORK IN 1983 TO LAUNCH AN EXTENSIVE VIDEO TRAINING PROGRAMME OF OVER 150 TITLES.

A DECADE LATER, THEY OPENED A THIRD LONDON SALON - THE CLUB, IN COUNTY HALL ON THE BANKS OF THE THAMES. APPOINTED CREATIVE DIRECTOR OF HEAD & SHOULDERS, THE UK'S TOP ANTI-DANDRUFF SHAMPOO IN 1998, BEVERLY SHORTLY AFTERWARDS BECAME THE FIRST HAIRDRESSER TO CREATE A DAY SPA SALON, COBELLA AKQA, OFFERING HIGH-TECH, TAILORED HAIR AND BEAUTY TREATMENTS TO MEN AND WOMEN, A STEP THAT WAS GENERALLY REGARDED A MAJOR CONTRIBUTION TO BRITISH HAIRDRESSING.

Even greater success followed. Two years later Beverly became the first woman to win the Oscar of the hairdressing world - British Hairdresser of the Year. Having won the accolade two years running, and with a glamorous TV profile, she's at the pinnacle of her career. "Winning British Hairdresser of the Year was the highlight of my life - after having my children," she says.

That same year, Anestis put his business acumen to the test in transforming The World Hairdressing Congress, the 25-year-old international hair styling event, into The Hair Congress - one of the most influential events in the hairdressing world. Held annually at the Grosvenor Hotel on Park Lane, it features a unique line-up of hand-picked celebrity hair stylists, fashion designers and famous faces.

I recall being impressed by Beverly's talent as I passed pins and watched her mind tick as she prepared for the Alternative Hair Show at the Albert Hall three years ago. No other woman has achieved so much in hairdressing. She is an inspiration - living proof that you can achieve anything if you try hard enough.

The dynamic pair opened their fourth salon in 2004 on the third floor at Selfridges, London, less than a year after realising their ultimate ambition of launching their own stylish haircare and styling range - The Cobella Collection.

Beverly was in her final year as the first female president of the Fellowship for British Hairdressing when I photographed her, looking so beautiful as always. The sun was still shining, but on the wrong side of the house. After choosing three locations, I felt we had the shot that reflected these two icons - one hairdresser, one businessman who, together, make for a great partnership.

2004: Cobella salon opens in Selfridges, London

2003: The Cobella Collection launches

2002: Beverly awarded British Hairdresser of the Year
Beverly appointed President of the Fellowship for British
Hairdressing
Anestis takes over The World Hairdressing Congress

2001: Beverly awarded British Hairdresser of the Year

1999: Cobella Akqa day spa opens

1998: Beverly appointed Creative Director of Head & Shoulders

1997: The Club opens

1987, 1988: Joint London Stylist of the Year

1979: Cobella Avant Garde Hair by Anestis Cobella published

BORN AND RAISED IN THE EAST END OF LONDON, RAYMOND BEGAN HIS HAIRDRESSING APPRENTICESHIP IN 1956, AT THE TENDER AGE OF 13. FROM JOHN OF LANSDOWNE PLACE HE WENT TO WORK FOR RAYMOND "TEASIE WEASIE" BESSONE ON BROMPTON ROAD, WHERE HIS CLIENTS INCLUDED DIGNITARIES SUCH AS BEAUTY EDITOR, SHIRLEY LORD.

IN 1964, AGED 20, HE EMIGRATED TO AMERICA WHERE ON HIS SECOND DAY ON NEW YORK'S STREETS HE CHANCED UPON PAUL MITCHELL WHO'D RECENTLY BEEN APPOINTED STYLE DIRECTOR OF HENRI BENDEL AT 10 WEST 57TH STREET. THE VERY SAME DAY RAYMOND HIMSELF BECAME A HENRI BENDEL EMPLOYEE.

Four years later, Raymond opened his own salon with friend Nasser with a staff of seven. Within two years, a team of 27 occupied the basement, ground-floor and mezzanine of a new $700,000, 6,500 square feet salon on 747 Madison Avenue, where the peach terrazzo floors and mirrored ceilings earned them a beauty industry design award. "We designed magnificent peach gowns for the ladies, and purple ones for the men. We were the first and hippest full service beauty salon of the day," says Raymond.

If there was one thing that Raymond learnt from Teasie Weasie, it was the art of service. Once collected from their private jet, Raymond and Nasser's international clientele had at their disposal 30 hairdressers, 10 manicurists, 10 assistants, three skin-care specialists, six colourists, four makeup artists, four maids, three receptionists and two appointment-takers and a retired NYC detective providing security. Every day, from midday to 3.30pm, a French lady prepared four types of lunch, served on the finest English bone china. "You could arrive at 9am and leave at 9 o'clock at night; there was no limit to the pampering," recalls Raymond, whose own daily routine included a couple of hours in the Plaza Hotel doing Betty Davis' hair.

Raymond learnt another invaluable lesson from Teasie Weasie, the pursuit of which got him arrested, twice. Achieving national press coverage for the new salon proved tough until Raymond master-minded two stories. The first was when he wanted to publicise the new mod cut that was blown just with the blow dryer. He persuaded a top agency to lend him 20 models for free, took them to an ice rink in the middle of which he and his team dressed out a mini salon and cut hair until the police arrived. The next time, he tried harder - he recreated a salon on the runway of the local airport. Somewhat eccentric, but the headlines followed.

LIKE PAUL MITCHELL, SCOTT WAS BORN IN SCOTLAND, TRAINED BY VIDAL SASSOON, AND EVENTUALLY MOVED TO THE UNITED STATES "FOR A BETTER LIFE". THERE HE SET UP COLORCUTTINGUSA, AN EDUCATION COMPANY IN ARIZONA, OFFERING COURSES, VIDEO EDUCATION AND TOOLS OF THE TRADE.

With business partner Linda Yodice, Scott teaches how and why colour works, believing the best way to bring out a stylist's ability and creativity is to lift their self-esteem. The principles underlining his teachings can be found in articles in magazines such as Elle, Modern Salon, Ladies Home Journal and Studio magazines. In 2003, the industry recognised his talent by awarding him HaircolorUSA Hair Colorist of the Year.

Opened in 1985, the Scott Cole salon is recognised as one of the top in the country. Who does he thank for his success? "Many people come to mind, but there are defining moments in my life for which the following individuals are responsible for: my mother who steered me towards Vidal Sassoon', Vidal himself, my wife who brings order to my chaos, and Jean Paul Dejoria, an ongoing inspiration."

Every hairdresser has an amusing client story. Julia Childs, who cried every time he cut her hair, is Scott's pick. "When I politely suggested she try another hairdresser, she was adamant that she actually loved her hair and myself, and crying was the way she expressed it. This went on for years and she never got any better," he recalls.

These days Scott divides his time between his salon in Atlanta, Georgia, his academy in Carefree, Arizona, and the artistic directorship for John Paul Mitchell Systems' The Color. Goals for 2004 include opening a further two schools. Although slowly shifting his focus towards education, Scott knows at heart that he's a haircutter, and that the salon will always be part of his life.

I had arranged to meet him on Broadway, where he was preparing for the International Beauty Show. Once I'd photographed him, I went to see Scott perform on the platform. His colouring ideas and techniques were extraordinary; the finished jobs were amongst the best I have seen in the USA. When will we see Scott Cole in Europe?

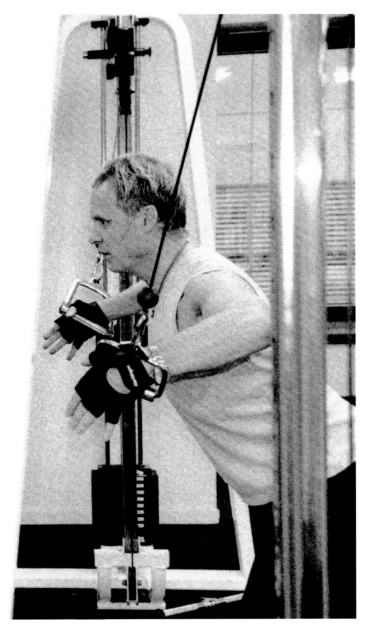

2003: HaircolorUSA Hair Colorist of the Year
2002: HaircolorUSA Most Innovative Techniques
1993: NAHA Multi-Cultural Hairdresser of the Year
1978: Emigrated to America

THERE ARE FEW AREAS OF THE HAIRDRESSING INDUSTRY THAT HAVE NOT BENEFITED FROM THE INFLUENCE AND EXPERTISE OF ANDREW COLLINGE. A WORKING HAIRDRESSER AT THE CUTTING EDGE OF HIS INDUSTRY, HE IS ONE OF THE MOST HIGHLY RESPECTED FIGURES IN THE BUSINESS.

HIS SUCCESSFUL SALON BUSINESS - THE LATEST AT SELFRIDGES IN MANCHESTER - SHOWS, EXHIBITIONS, MAGAZINE SHOOTS AND HIS HAIRCARE RANGE, KEEP HIM AS BUSY AS HE'S EVER BEEN DURING HIS 25 YEARS IN HAIRDRESSING.

When the British Government established the official authority to oversee standards in the hair and beauty industry (HABIA) Andrew, already an international ambassador for the trade, was made its honorary president which involved him attending the National Skills Festival hosted by Prince Charles at St James' Palace.

Twice British Hairdresser of the Year, and International Hairdresser of the Year, in 1996 Andrew followed his father, Peter Collinge, as president of the Fellowship for British Hairdressing, held the role in 1974, the year that Andrew started hairdressing.

Ten salons in the Northwest of England serve more than 2000 clients a week and his Academy in Liverpool is internationally respected as a major training centre. The Academy is a family affair - Peter is chairman, Andrew managing director, while his sister Sarah and wife Liz are directors. Supporting them is a loyal workforce of over 200 staff, many of whom have been with the company for several years.

Andrew was very much a pioneer in the early years of hairdressing on television. With Liz, he performed over 500 makeovers during their nine years on the daytime TV show This Morning. More recently, the couple were seen on Icons on Channel 4, recreating the looks of Hollywood legends.

In recent years Andrew has enjoyed a busy international agenda, travelling four continents hosting highly acclaimed stage shows such as World Hair Berlin 2002 and 2000 Le Mondial Coiffure in Paris. Andrew's honour in styling the hair of Sophie Countess of Wessex on the day of her marriage led to an invitation to himself and Liz as guests at the wedding and the reception at Windsor Castle.

Andrew forecasts that as our lives become busier, hairdressers will be expected to adapt and create more versatile styles. "We will need to manage hair easily and change styles frequently," he says. "Haircare and colour products will advance technically and play a bigger part in everybody's haircare routine".

In 1993 Andrew launched his own product range called Salon Solutions, now an established brand in the UK and overseas. Liz, meanwhile, sells her own equally successful cosmetics line in Boots and Andrew Collinge salons.

Andrew and I met very early in the morning at the front doors of Harrods, where he used to have a long hair salon on the fifth floor. "Harold, you have ten minutes to shoot," he told me, so one, two, three on the ready I took some shots right there before rushing into Hyde Park, my standby location. The last I saw of him Andrew was hotfooting it to Buckingham Palace. What a life.

2002: Opens salon in Selfridges, Trafford Centre, Manchester
2000: International Hairdresser of the Year
     AIPP Grand Trophy
     Best Haircut Award, Hair magazine
1998: Image of the Year Award
1997: British Hairdresser of the Year
1996: President, Fellowship for British Hairdressing
1993: British Hairdresser of the Year
     Launches Andrew Collinge Salon Solutions

CLIVE IS ONE OF THE REBELLIOUS MEN OF OUR INDUSTRY. I HAD A GUT FEELING WATCHING HIM AT THE 1987 ALTERNATIVE HAIR SHOW. HE WAS TALL, DARK, HANDSOME, A BLACKBELT IN MARTIAL ARTS AND HAD "CRISIS EQUALS OPPORTUNITY" TATTOOED IN JAPANESE ON HIS RIGHT ARM - NEED I SAY MORE? I EVENTUALLY MET HIM ON MY PAUL MITCHELL TRAVELS, SINCE WHEN I'VE THOUGHT OF HIM AS THE MOST FEARLESS MAN I KNOW.

His creative show input is amazing; he comes up with a winning hairstyle year by year. When you work up-close with the Clives of this world, you realise what individuals are really made of. We musn't lose sight of the fact that models are just good looking girls who've answered an ad in the paper. The rest is up to Clive and his team. You can't afford a hangover on show weekends - Clive certainly never had one.

It must be his healthy hobbies that keep him at the top of his field. Actually, I know it is because his advice to those who wish to follow in his footsteps is: "Work hard and study some form of relaxation to replenish your mind." He practices yoga every week with his wife, Kelly, and their two sons.

Now in his late 40s, Clive started hairdressing at the age of 12 on Brick Lane in London's East End. He moved onto a formal apprenticeship at Vidal Sassoon on Bond Street where he soon qualified as a stylist and at 19 became the youngest ever Sassoon manager. "My first impression of Vidal was that the guy was like a movie star," recalls Clive. He was later transferred to run the company's Dusseldorf operation.

Clive worked with Sassoon for a total of 11 years before opening his own salon in Maastricht, Holland. After five years, he headed back to the UK where he founded Burlingtons, his current British operation, which now employs around 30 staff. Plans for 2004 include breaking into American TV by aiming his Burlingtons product range at the 60 million viewers of the Home Shopping Network.

ROBERT CROMEANS IS MUCH RESPECTED AS AN EDUCATOR AND MOTIVATOR. CHARISMATIC, AND ALWAYS THE WILD ONE OF THE BUNCH, HIS TYPICALLY WITTY MOTTO IS: "IF AT FIRST YOU DO SUCCEED, TRY NOT TO LOOK SO BLOODY SURPRISED!"

BORN IN GLASGOW, HE MOVED TO THE UNITED STATES IN 1985, WHERE HE WAS SNAPPED UP BY THE LEGENDARY JEANNE BRAA FOR JOHN PAUL MITCHELL SYSTEMS, AND QUICKLY ESTABLISHED HIMSELF IN THE BRIGHT LIGHTS OF THE PROFESSIONAL BEAUTY INDUSTRY. BASED IN SAN DIEGO, HE APPEARED ON STAGE FOR JPMS NATIONALLY AND INTERNATIONALLY AND TODAY, AS ARTISTIC DIRECTOR CONTINUES TO MOTIVATE HAIRDRESSERS WORLDWIDE.

Paul Mitchell and Robert had a lot more in common than being Scots - a drive to be the best and a delight in the company of women was typical of both men.

Robert's list of accomplishments includes inventing the ARCS scissors, creating ponytail haircutting, form cutting, teased highlighting, forking and stapling, and a highlighting and colouring technique using chopsticks.

In 1995, Robert and his wife Margaret opened the first of two San Diego salons, one of which features a Colour Bar beneath a million dollar glass dome, whilst the other has been turned into a Paul Mitchell cosmetology school. They own other salons in Las Vegas and Los Angeles, all staffed by a hand-picked group of talented individuals trained by Robert himself. "Since I usually work in my own salon, three days a week, I speak to them as a peer, not as a teacher, removed from the real business of working behind a chair," he says.

Four years ago, Robert made a Paul Mitchell commercial with the tag line 'Your hairdresser can do anything!' "Everybody feels they have the worst hair; our job is to reverse that. That commercial defined my career," admits the three times Platform Artist of the Year. Seen worldwide in these commercials, he is frequently invited to make guest appearances on television and radio.

When I met him in New York in early 2003, I was told that we had half an hour to get the shots. We wandered through Brooklyn searching for a good location, when a huge jockey pants billboard declaring 'The Next Best Thing to Naked' grabbed my attention. Having seen girls swoon, watching Robert on stage, I knew this was the right spot.

He has come a long way, but has yet to show off his daring designs in London. Continued good luck, Robert...

2003: Platform Artist of the Year,
      Behindthechair.com' s Stylists Choice Awards
2002: Platform Artist of the Year,
2001: Platform Artist of the Year,

RENOWNED FOR CLASSIC STYLING, ELEGANT CUTS AND THE BEST BLOW-DRYING AND POLISHED FINISHING IN LONDON, ERROL DOUGLAS' CREATIONS REGULARLY APPEAR IN THE STUNNING PHOTOGRAPHIC SPREADS OF VOGUE, HARPERS & QUEEN AND COSMOPOLITAN.

BEGINNING IN 1981 WITH AN APPRENTICESHIP AT NEVILLE DANIEL, THE HACKNEY-BORN TEENAGER GAINED EXPERIENCE IN ALL ASPECTS OF HAIR STYLING, FROM ART DIRECTING TO SESSION STYLING AT A NUMBER OF TOP LONDON SALONS.

Errol's salon in Knightsbridge, which opened in 1998, fuses two very different styles of hairdressing: European and Afro. "I'd never had a firm base and after many years of searching for the right environment Motcomb Street surpassed my greatest expectations," he says. It probably passes clients expectations too, with its beauty area, masseur, nail technician, in-house catering, chauffeur service, exclusive jewelry range, and even personalised umbrellas. Supporting him is a 41-strong staff of talented and creative stylists, many of whom have worked with him throughout his career.

Like many of his colleagues, Errol's priority is to make women look and feel their best, an aim he certainly achieves judging by the women he's helped make the most glamorous in the world - Iman, Helena Christiansen, Naomi Campbell and Cindy Crawford to name a few.

Errol regularly judges industry competitions and has been involved in National Hairdressing Awards in Australia, Holland, Japan and Spain. He is also a familiar face on the judging panel of the annual Wahl/Black Beauty & Hair Awards and the Fellowship for British Hairdressing Awards, as well as student competitions in colleges and training schools across the UK.

Errol's hairdressing talents, professionalism and exuberant personality make him a television natural. Early in his career, the father of three became a regular on the BBC Clothes Show, which led to his slot on the BBC's Style Challenge. Today, he's keen to develop a training school and photographic studio where he can share his extensive knowledge and skills. Maybe then this British creative figurehead will achieve his goal of winning British Hairdresser of the Year, for which he's been nominated seven times. Next time lucky?

2003: Ambassador of Hairdressing
2001: Black Men of Merit Recognition Award
2000: Fellowship for British Hairdressing Honours Award
1996: British Afro Hairdresser of the Year
      Babyliss Award
1995: London L'Oreal Colour Trophy
1994: British Afro Hairdresser of the Year
      Joined the Fellowship for British Hairdressing FAME Team

LAWRENCE STARTED HIS CAREER AT THE AGE OF 15 ON ERIC OF BAKER STREET WORKING ALONGSIDE A MASTERFUL HAIRDRESSER FROM THE OLD SCHOOL CALLED ERIC THALLON, A FOUNDER MEMBER OF THE FELLOWSHIP FOR BRITISH HAIRDRESSING.

SIX YEARS LATER, LAWRENCE BOUGHT THE SALON, RENAMED IT CRIMPERS AND TRANSFORMED IT INTO THE WORLD'S FIRST UNISEX SALON.

"The very first thing we did was include men's hairdressing next to our ladies. We also did away with the standard regulations of wearing a shirt and tie, and played music. This was the 1960s; rules needed to be broken", explains Lawrence. "We decided to never blow dry unless we had first cut a client's hair ourselves, even if it meant turning them away, in order to prove what a superior cut they would have compared to anything they'd known before." "Crimpers was also the first salon not to display the owners name above the door."

International fame followed. The world's press turned up to report on this British phenomenon, where men and women had their hair styled sitting next to each other in unaccustomed proximity - "Quelle Revolution!" opined Paris Match.

Today, Lawrence lives in Antibes in the south of France with his talented wife Jhaleh and family, having sold his share in Crimpers International in 1992. Far from retiring, he continues to create beautiful hair for film and advertising.

THE FELLOWSHIP FOR BRITISH HAIRDRESSING WAS FOUNDED IN 1946 AS THE FELLOWSHIP OF HAIR ARTISTS OF GREAT BRITAIN. A FOUNDING MEMBER OF THE ORGANISATION ARTISTIQUE INTERNATIONALE - THE WORLD AUTHORITY FOR HAIRDRESSING COMPETITIONS - ATTRACTED THE INDUSTRY'S BEST FROM THE OUTSET. MEMBERSHIP HAS ALWAYS BEEN BY INVITATION AND BESTOWS A PARTICULAR STATUS ON INDIVIDUAL MEMBERS AND SALONS.

A LIFE MEMBER, I JOINED WAY BACK IN THE 1950S. I REMEMBER AS A YOUNG LAD AT DUMAS WHEN OUR BOSS, FRANK BLASCHKE, WAS MADE PRESIDENT OF THE FELLOWSHIP - VIDAL SASSOON, GERARD LONDON AND I WERE CONSIDERED HIGH FLYERS BECAUSE WE WORKED FOR HIM. THE YOUNG UPSTARTS OF OUR DAY, JUST LIKE THE ADEE PHELANS AND LEE STAFFORDS OF TODAY, WE WERE OUT TO MAKE A NAME FOR OURSELVES, AND THE BEST WAY TO START WAS AT THE FELLOWSHIP.

By the 1980s, a new generation of hairdressers was emerging with style and priorities of their own. Stars like Vidal Sassoon and Trevor Sorbie set a different agenda, pioneering new levels of public awareness. Their membership of The Fellowship meant the organisation began to take on a renewed role as the bastion of quality in British hairdressing.

During Xavier Wenger's chairmanship, The Fellowship continued to flourish, both nationally and abroad. Low-key educational events became an increasingly important part of its activities, along with larger shows and showcase events. During this period, the Luncheon and Awards - the only major industry awards voted for exclusively by top hairdressers was also firmly established on the UK calendar.

Under the chairmanship of Christofer Mann, The Fellowship blossomed further into the high profile organisation it is today. Recognising a new breed of celebrity hairdresser, The Fellowship set out to live up to its newly-acquired motto, "Strength through Quality."

Soon, every high profile name and salon group was lining up to join this prestigious association. Important showcase events in London and around Britain gave members a unique opportunity to demonstrate their talents, whilst the Fellowship's highly successful Masterclass! educational events became an instant hit throughout the UK.

Launched in the early 1990s, the Fellowship Academy of Merit and Excellence (FAME) team aims to create a new generation of hairdressers. It has helped the careers of many of today's top hairdressers, amongst them Errol Douglas, Antoinette Beenders and the late Umberto Giannini. Today, competition for places is fierce.

Project X, The Fellowship's latest training initiative - under the guidance of John Carne - has achieved much since its launch in 2002. The syllabus was designed to hone the skills of hairdressing's most

promising young talent by offering unrivalled training with the UK's best hairdressers, and with the possibility of the outstanding students being put forward for selection for the FAME Team, Project X really can change the career destiny of young hairdressers.

Monday 28th July 2003 saw Fellowship members gathered at London's Albert Memorial for a shoot I'd been planning for at least 18 months with the support of "Jewel of the Fellowship", Ann Herman. What a fete of organisation - imagine trying to book Robbie Williams 70 times over - that's been my wonderful task. What a great bunch of people to pass on my comb and brush to.

I love going to the Fellowship meetings, the dos, the FAME nights. There are no events like them in America, so come on guys, let's get The Fellowship running in the USA.

I've always thought that The Fellowship doesn't get the credit it deserves, but when I read the membership list I realised that there was all the credit it could need. When I see all this talent on Britain's high streets I can't help feeling a surge of pride for British hairdressing. The public, the personalities, the celebrities all are lucky - our standard is the highest. But we mustn't be complacent - I say be creative, be aggressive. That's how we got to the top. And that's how we'll stay there.

MEMBER QUOTES

"The Fellowship represents the crème de la crème of British Hairdressing." BEVERLY COBELLA

"I'm immensely proud to have been chairman of The Fellowship at an important period in its history. I believe we have carried forward our message of "Strength through Quality" to an increasing number of members and to the industry." STEPHEN MESSIAS

"The Fellowship is the single most important industry organisation in the UK of which I'm proud to be a member." NICKY CLARKE

"I'm proud to be a Patron of The Fellowship, an organisation that continues to achieve great things for British hairdressing."
TREVOR SORBIE

"Watching the amazing young talent that continues to be nurtured by the Fellowship with Masterclass!, F.A.M.E. and Project X is what keeps me inspired and helps maintain a young outlook on the industry."
ANN HERMAN

"We continue to support and encourage our team to participate at Fellowship events wherever possible because it is a truly great organisation." CHARLES WORTHINGTON

"Ultimately, if you want to get ahead in hairdressing in the UK you have to become a member of The Fellowship. It's that influential."
CHRISTOFER MANN

"As a former member of the F.A.M.E. Team I have been responsible for the team for the last couple of years. I do it because it's important to develop young talent and to give back a little of what I was privileged to enjoy as a member." SEAN DAWSON

"I was delighted to be a president of The Fellowship partly because my father was a president before me, but also because I believe in everything the organisation stands for." ANDREW COLLINGE

"The Fellowship gave me a Most Promising award at the very start of my career. I continue to support the work of this outstanding body because its role is more important now than ever before."
ANTHONY MASCOLO

"I support the Fellowship because it's all about quality and passion for the craft of hairdressing. It plays an important, some would say essential, role in maintaining the traditions that have made British hairdressing the best in the world." VIDAL SASSOON

I've known Simon since Paul Mitchell introduced us in 1985. I accompanied him to Antenna in Kensington, but the salon was small, so I left them to it. Some two hours later I popped in again to see how Paul was. There he was with his short haircut, and now a long ponytail. In those days hair extensions were new. These days, wearing them is like having breakfast, except breakfast can cost £25 in a smart hotel, and extensions can set you back thousands for a complete headfull. Proof of Simon's success can be seen everywhere, on the heads of A-list stars such as singer Kylie, Victoria Beckham, Britney Spears, and members of the public alike. The industry tills are singing sweet songs, thanks to him. Well done, Simon.

He tells a story from the early 80s about the night Boy George got locked in Antenna with the salon ghost. The singer's only way out was through the ceiling doors. Just as he was lowering his frame down the front of the building, a passing policeman helped George to the ground, saying: "Careful, madam. We really don't want to hurt you" - the title, of course, of his then current hit single.

Simon is chairman of Dome Cosmetics Ltd, an international manufacturing and distribution company exclusively supplying the professional market with Monofibre and related products. Established in 1986, it is the world's number one hair extension company, with headquarters in London, a wholly-owned American subsidiary in Atlanta, USA and Köln in Germany, and distributors trading under the Dome brand in 25 other countries.

As you can see, these days, Simon expresses his creativity with a blow torch instead of a blow dryer! London's prestigious Institute of Contemporary Arts and the Victoria & Albert Museum have both exhibited his metal sculptures. A great admirer of Picasso, it wouldn't surprise me if he were to swap his hairbrush for a paintbrush, too. A wild man with a great personality, he looks like a warrior ready for the salon.

SIMON FORBES; WHAT A GENIUS TO HAVE INVENTED HAIR EXTENSIONS. HIS INNOVATIVE CONTRIBUTION WAS OFFICIALLY ACKNOWLEDGED WHEN HE WON THE FELLOWSHIP FOR BRITISH HAIRDRESSING MILLENNIUM AWARD IN 2000, THE SAME YEAR HE SET ABOUT REVOLUTIONISING THE HAIR COLOURING MARKET WITH PROLIN HAIR ENHANCERS.

"IT TOOK 15 YEARS FOR HAIR EXTENSIONS TO BE ACCEPTED AS A SERIOUS SALON SERVICE. BUT IT WAS WORTH EVERY EFFORT," SAYS SIMON. "PROLIN IS A NEW CHEMICAL-FREE CONCEPT THAT WILL ALSO CONQUER THE TRADE IN YEARS TO COME."

2000: Invented Prolin hair enhancers
       Fellowship for British Hairdressing
       Millennium Award
1994: President of the Fellowship of Hair
       Artists of Great Britain
1991: Alternative Hairdresser of the Year
1986: Established Dome Cosmetics Ltd.
1980: Invented Monofibre hair extensions
       and founded Antenna
1965: Career starts with an apprenticeship

Photo: John Cole

French of London 1949

AT THE HEART OF BRITISH FASHION REVOLUTION OF THE 1960S WAS A REMARKABLE MAN WHO HAD THE COURAGE TO LEAD THE WAY IN HAIR DESIGN, THEN THE LEAST REPORTED ASPECT OF FASHION. THE NAME WAS FREDDY FRENCH, ONE OF THE FIRST TO UNDERSTAND THE POWER OF THE MEDIA TO DISSEMINATE NEW IDEAS.

IN SORRY I KEPT YOU WAITING MADAM, VIDAL SASSOON WRITES: "I USED TO WATCH FREDDY AT THE ACADEMY [OF HAIRDRESSING]. I WOULD STAND THERE ENTHRALLED, BUT I AM SORRY TO SAY I WAS ONE OF THE FEW WHO UNDERSTOOD WHAT HE WAS DOING. HE WAS SO NEW, SO UTTERLY DIFFERENT THAT SOME OF THE AUDIENCE LAUGHED, WHICH USED TO MAKE ME FURIOUS. THEY DID NOT REALISE THAT HERE WAS THE MAN WHO WOULD CHANGE HAIRDRESSING."

From the early 1930s to the late 60s, French of London led the way in hair fashion, freeing hairdressing from its former rigidity with his breakthrough casual hairstyle, Designed Disorder. Perhaps his most significant achievement was spreading an awareness and appreciation of hairdressing as an art by collaborating with great photographers, amongst them Cecil Beaton, Norman Eales and John Cole. His extensive collection of hair and fashion photographs is probably one of the best there is.

Freddy's seminal contribution to the industry has not gone unacknowledged. He was the first hairdresser to receive the Beaverbrook Award for Outstanding Service to the Fashion Industry - was presented with the Cartier Award for Most Progressive Hair Designer of the last 35 years; and his presidency of Intercoiffure, the international association of prestige hairdressers, spanned six years.

One Monday, at the start of my career, I attended the Academy on Charlotte Street to see the man I had read about in the hairdressers' bible, Hairdressers Journal, a pink little book in those days. As I waited amongst the standing mirrors and dressing tables, I saw this short man with a mass of hair and a check suit come in to a round of applause. Without further ado, Mr French showed his work to the hundred or so assembled members.

His hairstyles, softer than we had been taught until then, were created using an unusual brush, which eventually became known as the wooden-handled Denman - a hairdresser's number one tool. Stylish, charismatic, and ahead of his time, Freddy was a star.

Years later, when consulting for Glemby International, I befriended his charming son, Nicholas, who has established his own creative authority on both sides of the Atlantic, working the international stage with magical contemporary interpretations of his father's elegant styles.

Photo: Joseph Cartright

AT THE START OF MY CAREER, I MET AN EXCEPTIONALLY TALENTED, STYLISH MAN BY THE NAME OF FREDDY FRENCH - THE SORT OF MAN WHOM EVERYONE LOOKED UP TO. WHEN HE APPEARED, CLAD IN A TWEED SUIT AND BOW TIE, AT THE CHARLOTTE STREET ACADEMY ON A MONDAY EVENING, HE WAS THE ONE TO WATCH. FREDDY, STEINER AND TEASIE WEASIE WERE THE FORERUNNERS OF 60S FASHION HAIRDRESSING.

THEN, WHEN I WAS CONSULTING FOR GLEMBY INTERNATIONAL IN THE MID-70S, A YOUNG MAN JOINED THE CREATIVE TEAM. IT WASN'T UNTIL WEEKS LATER THAT HE TOLD ME HIS SURNAME - IT WAS AT THIS POINT THAT I REALISED HE WAS NICKY FRENCH, FREDDY'S SON, AND HIS GREATEST ADMIRER.

"My father rose from poverty to the highest echelons of society, single-handedly beginning the Casual Hairdressing movement along the way," says Nicky. Freddy's collection of wonderful photos in and on the covers of Vogue, Harpers & Queen and Tatler from the 1940s to the 1970s is his most treasured possession.

Nicky's specialty is producing exciting hair shows and unique designs for the big and the small screen. He's done catwalk shows for the likes of Emanuel Ungaro, Levi and Betsey Johnson, and worked with celebrated film directors, such as Ridley Scott and Adrien Lyne.

Speaking of fashion, Nicky says: "Hair fashion forecasts are recognised from fashion intelligence, and developed from the "runway to reality." Individuality is the key; versatility is the outcome. Many [future] catwalks will show smooth, curly, wavy hair, but the public will stay hooked on smooth, fresh-looking, coloured hair. The minority youth cultures will still have that stop-look! aspect. Their hair will have extremely avant-garde silhouettes seasonally with a mix of extreme colour."

America loves Nicky. As well as being voted one of the top 70 Educators of the Century by Modern Salon magazine, he's performed six times at the Alternative Hair Show both in the UK and America.

Carol, a model of mine from the 70s, is now Nicky's wife and personal assistant, organising all his shows, seminars, travel and photographic assignments. I guess sleeping with his co-director and secretary is the only way Nicky can keep up with his workload as a design team leader and spokesperson of Matrix, one of the leading brands of professional hair products worldwide.

I last saw him on stage at the International Beauty Show in New York. What an inspiration: Nicky is one of that rare breed that successfully follow in their father's footsteps - and go one better.

JOHN IS ONE OF THE MOST PROLIFIC HAIRDRESSERS OF HIS TIME. BORN IN 1951, HE LEFT SCHOOL AT 16 TO LAND A JOB AS A JUNIOR FOR THE LEGENDARY LEONARD LEWIS.

"WHEN I WANT TO DO SOMETHING, NO ONE CAN CHANGE MY MIND, AND I DECIDED TO BE THE BEST ASSISTANT LEONARD HAD EVER HAD," RECALLS JOHN. "IF I SWEPT THE FLOOR, IT WAS GOING TO BE THE CLEANEST FLOOR. EVERYBODY HATED FOLDING TOWELS, BUT TO ME IT BECAME AN OBSESSION."

Almost immediately, he assisted Leonard on shoots for Vogue, and so began a strong marriage between master and pupil. Magazines began booking John himself to style the hair of stars from Jackie O' to Jerry Hall. In 1975, he opened his flagship salon in London's West End and went on a year later to create the cut that made his name - Joanna Lumley's sleek pageboy bob for The Avengers.

John's quality of work has consistently shone through in his three London salons over the last 20 years, coming to fruition in the creation of Ready-to-Wear, his first signature haircare and styling range line, launched in 1988. When he demonstrated the products on This Morning the TV station's switchboard jammed. Boots' next order was for 1.2 million bottles of Thickening Lotion and 860,000 jars of wax.

John notched up another first in 1998 with his Sheer Blonde range - tailored to every shade from platinum to honey - and four years later, he collaborated with Sally Hershberger on another groundbreaking success, Beach Blonde.

In 2002, the John Frieda product empire was sold to the Japanese Kao Corporation for a reportedly phenomenal £600m - the highest figure ever reached by the sale of a private hairdressing business. One of its brands, Frizz-Ease Serum, remains the No. 1 styling product on both sides of the Atlantic, breaking the sales sound barrier and outshining every product on the market. The Evening Standard declared later that year that John was "now the country's highest earner", while the Sunday Times included him in their Rich List of Britain's 1000 wealthiest people. In 2003, John's £167million fortune placed him at no. 189. "Maybe I've been lucky," he says, "but my father always used to say: the harder you work, the luckier you get."

Sadly, John is the only hairdresser and friend that I could not persuade to pose in front of my camera. In the picture opposite, taken in 1998, he's with my friends Michael Rasser, Vidal Sassoon, Nicky Clarke and the man this night was honouring, Leonard.

WHEN HAIR COLOURING BEGAN TO FLOURISH IN THE EARLY 1970S ONE NAME WAS TALKED ABOUT INCESSANTLY - DANIEL GALVIN. A NEW BREED OF COLOURIST, HE OPENED UP A WORLD OF FUN IN HAIRDRESSING.

I REMEMBER IT WELL; MY COLOURIST AT HARRODS WOULD PLAY WITH VIBRANT REDS, BLUES, GREENS AND ORANGES WHERE PREVIOUSLY ALL WE HAD TO WORK WITH WAS BLONDE HIGHLIGHTS PROCESSED WITH SILVER FOIL.

2003: Transforms salon into a super-salon
2000: Fellowship for British Hairdressing Film Award for A
    Clockwork Orange
1990s: Launches own range of professional and retail hair
    colouring products
1987: Refurbishes his salon
1978: Intercoiffure Award for Most Promising Young Hair Designer
1970s: Opens salon on George Street, the first to specialise in colour
    Develops the Slicing Technique
    Develops Natural Lights and Three-Tone Highlights
1960s: Creates Crazy Colour
    Joins Leonard of Mayfair

Daniel began colouring in the 60s as director of colour at the large tinting department of the legendary Leonard of Mayfair. There he developed and refined his ideas that would soon become a life's work. Specialisation in colour was a new area in hairdressing, most of us preferring to cut and style. It's fair to say that Daniel has helped pioneer every major innovation in hair colouring techniques, and their application, since colour took on a life of its own. No other colourist can claim responsibility for half the Japanese population, some 63 million people, dying their hair.

Daniel remains the King of Colour, continuing to work five-days a week at his London salon, counting amongst regular clients Madonna, Catherine Zeta-Jones, Richard Gere and Nicole Kidman. It was he that was responsible for the subtle hair transformation of the Princess of Wales during the 90s and for techniques and fashions such as Crazy Colour, Brickwork, Tip and Halo highlighting, Alice Band flashes, and Natural, Tinted and Tortoiseshell lights.

A life-long dream was realised in 2003, with the refurbishment into a super-salon of the George Street salon he opened three decades ago. A 9,000sq ft palace dedicated to colour, it has a bar, restaurant, beauty treatment areas, and a 40ft waterfall. "I feel about hair colour the way some people feel about golf. It's what I want to do until I die," says Daniel.

With three gifted children - Louise, James and Daniel Jr - working for him, the world is sure to be talking about the Galvins for decades to come.

Joshua left the Navy to start hairdressing in a Mayfair salon, before crossing the Atlantic to work for Revlon in New York, then returning to London in time for the swinging 60s, when he worked alongside Vidal Sassoon. In 1974, he formed Joshua Galvin London, and later a training academy and is known around the world for his teaching and as a compere at the Alternative Hair Show.

Nowadays, Joshua spends his time on product development, training young hairdressers and working one day a week at his brother Daniel's super-salon, where A-list celebrities such as Madonna and Nicole Kidman book an appointment when they're in town.

I have spent some good times with Joshua over the years, and recall especially the day he brought to my home a vast selection of hair pictures; I never knew his photography went so far back. If I'd gone to his office, I could have been there for days. It was only when we sat and talked about our yesterdays that I realised quite how much he'd achieved. "Fifty years on, I love hairdressing more than when I started," he says.

With so much to choose from it was a hard job selecting two shots that summarise his career. I chose John Swannell's work because I felt it complemented my own. Joshua's work has changed so much over the years that the new generation of hairdressers probably wouldn't remember these reprints. It was good to look over styles he no longer seems to do. We all change and grow.

I felt Josh's portrait should reflect his role as The Godfather of hairdressing, a role left vacant by Xavier Wenger. My friend Mario loaned me the old Ford Pilot, and I borrowed a black hat. Josh looks a bit like a member of the Mafia, but the props gave him the character I was after.

Photo: John Swannell

PART OF A FOUR GENERATION HAIRDRESSING DYNASTY, JOSHUA HAS BEEN IN THE BUSINESS FOR HALF A CENTURY, AND IN HIS TIME HAS LOOKED AFTER TRUE LEGENDS SUCH AS JUDY GARLAND AND MARY QUANT.

FOR 16 YEARS, HE FLEW TO PARIS EVERY FEW WEEKS TO CUT THE HAIR OF BALLERINA ZIZI JEANMAIRE FOR WHAT MUST HAVE BEEN AMONGST THE MOST EXPENSIVE CUTS OF ALL TIME.

Photo: Andrew O'Toole

THE SUDDEN DEATH OF UMBERTO GIANNINI SHOCKED THE HAIRDRESSING INDUSTRY TO ITS CORE. CHARISMATIC AND AFFABLE, HE WILL NEVER BE FORGOTTEN BY THE MANY HE INSPIRED.

UMBERTO'S RISE TO THE VERY TOP OF HIS VOCATION BEGAN AT 15 WORKING AS A SATURDAY BOY IN HIS UNCLE'S WORCESTER SALON. HAVING DISCOVERED HIS PASSION, HE PURSUED IT AT COLLEGE, AND LATER AT THE PAUL EDMONDS SALON IN LONDON, BEFORE RETURNING TO THE MIDLANDS IN 1988 TO SET UP HIS OWN IN KIDDERMINSTER. TODAY, TEN SALONS CARRY HIS NAME.

"Umberto was an inspiration to every young hairdresser. His ambition and hard work were rewarded with huge success, but it's his friendship that I miss the most." SEAN HANNA

"Umberto was a gentleman. I had a lot of respect for him as a person and the empire that grew from his talents. His death is a great loss to the industry and all of us who were lucky enough to be his friends or family." TREVOR SORBIE

"Umberto was one of the industry's good guys, an exceptionally talented individual in all aspects of hairdressing." PAUL STAFFORD

"Words could never describe the loss. Umberto will never be forgotten." LISA SHEPERD

"Umberto was a man with a mission who achieved so much, but left us with so much more to give." ANESTIS AND BEVERLY COBELLA

It was at Paul Edmonds' that Umberto befriended fellow icon-to-be Errol Douglas. "I remember being together at the British Hairdressing Awards when he turned to me and said: "I'm sure we can do that." From that moment, Umberto's motivation to succeed has had an unswerving influence on me," says Errol.

While designing and building the flagship Birmingham salon in 1996, he fell in love with Claire Shread. Together, they formulated and designed both his signature haircare range and Osis, a line of styling products for Schwarzkopf, of which Umberto at the time was creative director.

Umberto's philosophy of making women look as sexy as possible permeated his work, in particular his commercial haircuts and clever, yet simple styling seen on the beautiful heads of celebrities such as Kylie and Gisele Bunchden. His aesthetic sensibilities and love of fashion were typical of his Italian heritage. "Umberto truly loved and was inspired by all the beautiful things in life, from fashion to food," says Claire.

Tragically, Umberto was cut down in his prime. At just 33, he unexpectedly died from dermatomyositis, leaving behind Claire, their two young children and a host of friends and admirers. "Umberto always had a plan. His motivation was like no other person you'll ever meet - he always did what he set out to do," says Claire.

Under Claire's control the Umberto Giannini brand has become the fourth largest haircare brand in UK and exported worldwide. "The character of our products is very much Umberto - the focus is on glamour and the end look, rather than being a prescriptive range," explains Claire. One of her ambitions is to make the brand a meaningful force in Italy.

"Umberto was very much a leader by inspiration rather than authority. The fact that all the current franchise owners trained with him is a reflection of the loyalty he inspired," says Claire. "The essence of his hairdressing lives on through the salons."

2001: Umberto passed away on 11th January
2000: Curl friends and GUNK launched
      Worcester salon opens
1999: British Hairdresser of the Year
      Men's Hairdresser of the Year
      Celebrity Hairdresser of the Year
      Knightsbridge and Bromsgrove salons open
      Hair Cosmetics launched in America
1998: Wolverhampton salon opens
      Hair Cosmetics launched

1997: Youngest hairdresser to enter the Hall of Fame
1996: Midlands Hairdresser of the Year
      Birmingham salon opens
1995: Midlands Hairdresser of the Year
1994: Avant Garde Hairdresser of the Year
      Umberto Giannini Training Academy opens
1993: Midlands Hairdresser of the Year
1991: Hagley and Stourbridge salons open
1988: First Umberto Giannini salon opens in Kidderminster

I KNEW THE NAME OF MICHAEL GORDON AS THE OWNER OF BUMBLE AND BUMBLE, ONE OF NEW YORK'S MOST SUCCESSFUL SALONS, BUT IT WAS ONLY IN MIAMI IN EARLY 2003 ON READING AN ARTICLE ON HIS BOOK HAIR HEROES THAT I LEARNT THAT HE COMES FROM LONDON AND WAS TRAINED BY RENÉ, PRINCESS MARGARET'S HAIRDRESSER IN THE 1960S.

The son of a hairdresser, he began his career at the age of 15 and by 21 he had encountered his first editorial work and become the youngest artistic director at London's Elizabeth Arden salon. Having opened his first salon with his brother in Johannesburg, Michael moved to New York City for his next challenge.

In 1977, Bumble and bumble opened its hip doors in a tiny space on 57th Street, in competition with Manhattan's top hairdressing names. Michael immediately began producing photos for magazines, feeling it was the best way to show the press what the company was about, and of demonstrating to his staff the calibre of work expected of them.

After only one year, Bumble and bumble was in Vogue's list of top 10 salons in New York City, and has remained a leader ever since. The young, upbeat team is heavily involved in the fashion world, creating looks including the now-famous razor-cut movement. Salon stylists design hair on more magazine covers and fashion spreads than any other team in the world. Each season the editorial team styles hair on catwalks for elite designers in New York, London, Milan and Paris.

When not managing the salon, Michael looks after the funky Bumble and bumble product collection. One of the most watched lines in haircare, it is sold at select US salons and retail locations worldwide, including Space.NK in London and Colette in Paris.

Michael was most charming when I visited him at his town house, where we discovered that we once worked around the corner from one another in London but never met, and that he dislikes having his picture taken. On the last roll of film he turned almost to camera - that's the shot you see opposite.

OF ALL THE FRIENDS WHO INFLUENCED MY CAREER, LESLIE WAS ONE OF THE MOST IMPORTANT. AND I IMAGINE MANY OTHERS SUCH AS VIDAL SASSOON, GERARD LONDON AND JEAN FAYE WOULD SAY THE SAME. WE TRAINED, JOKED AND CRIED TOGETHER, ALTHOUGH THE TEARS WERE USUALLY TEARS OF LAUGHTER.

I FIRST MET LESLIE, NOT LONG AFTER THE WAR IN 1949, AT THE AWARD-WINNING ROMAINE'S ON EDGWARE ROAD. I WAS A NAÏVE TEENAGER; HE WAS AN EX-PRISONER OF WAR WITH AN INFECTIOUS SENSE OF HUMOUR. RELEASED FROM NORTH AFRICA IN MAY 1945, HE WAS 26 WHEN HE RETURNED TO

BRITAIN AND SIGNED A THREE-YEAR £1 - A WEEK CONTRACT WITH THE HIGHLY-RESPECTED HAIRDRESSER, CHARLES PLUMRIDGE. EIGHT MONTHS LATER, CHARLES WAS DEAD AND LESLIE JOINED ROMAINE'S.

"It was an exciting era in hairdressing," he recalls. "Romaine's had a school every night when we worked on models and discussed the good and bad points of each cut. We weren't very happy with Harold's and he wanted to re-do it. By now gone 11pm, we argued it was too late. He began to cry, complaining that he wouldn't be able to sleep if he didn't get the style right. So Vidal and I stayed behind and let him re-do his work. He finished just before 2am. Harold was not quite 17-years-old."

Anyone who was keen to learn needed a manager like Leslie behind them. When it was time to work, you worked. When it was time to learn, your put your head down and you stayed behind and practised - no excuses.

"Leonard Stein loved hairdressing with a passion and instilled his exemplary attitude in all of us that had the pleasure of working with him," recalls Vidal.

Working in the salon at the time was a young lady - the winner of the Rosebowl and the Vacquenol Shield - Connie Baker, today's Leslie's wife. Made an offer they couldn't refuse, the couple toured Ireland in the late 1950s, demonstrating the fashionable Nickel cold perm. Within two years they were back in London where Leslie joined Andre Bernard, training hairdressers who owned their own salons. One in particular offered Leslie half of his business, Robert of Croydon.

"We became partners and eventually had ten salons," he recalls. All of which he eventually found too much, limiting the final years of his career to managing the Purley and Croydon salons. He remains the owner of the former, but having retired 15 years ago on the advice of his doctor, no longer works.

"I made so many good friends during my career," says Leslie. Highlights? "Winning the Chriscola and Spring Fashion Cups - happy days."

CONSIDERED ONE OF THE WORLD'S MOST INVENTIVE CONCEPTUAL HAIR STYLISTS, WHAT A WONDERFUL, LAID BACK MAN IS GUIDO PALAU. I HAD A PICTURE IN MY MIND OF WHAT HE LOOKED LIKE - TALL, THICK SET, WAVY HAIR, LIKE MICHAELANGELO'S DAVID.

How wrong I was. The first moment I set eyes on this man, I thought. "That's not him." Born in Dorset of English and Spanish parents, he has a beautiful Saxon face belying his rather incongruous Italian-sounding name. He turned up for our photoshoot at the Lux Bar on Hoxton Square in East London bang on 3pm, the agreed time. How gratifying when people are on time.

Often creating looks six months in advance, his radically expressive styles have been seen on catwalks of such diverse fashion houses as Versace, Marc Jacobs and Alexander McQueen. Working from the philosophy that hair should be styled with more thought than product, Guido's adventurous mind and adept fingers create hair styles that look good for the whole evening, rather than falling apart when the wind blows, or when the client puts her fingers through her hair.

He regularly works with leading fashion photographers such as David Sims, Mario Testino and Steven Meisel and is regularly featured in best-selling Italian, French, British and American magazines. His work with Kate Moss in the Sunday Times magazine gave us the real glamour of a woman in her true colours.

What I like about this shot of Guido was the easy approach to the picture - all I wanted was a typical London street. Walking along the west side of Hoxton Square, the graffiti-covered wall spoke out to Guido. This is the simplicity of this creative young man. I was touched by his thoughtfulness in bringing me a gift - a copy of his critically-acclaimed book Heads: Hair by Guido.

Photo: Colin Roy

BORN AND BRED IN PUTNEY, SOUTH LONDON, ANNIE BEGAN HER CAREER WITH VIDAL IN THE 1950S WHEN HE BOUGHT THE BOND STREET SALON IN WHICH SHE WORKED.

DECIDING TO SPECIALISE IN COLOUR AND PERMING SHE TURNED TO THE LABORATORY AND INVENTED COLOUR AND PERMING TECHNIQUES THAT ALLOWED WOMEN TO WEAR THEIR HAIR IN EASY-CARE STYLES THEY HADN'T EVEN DREAMT OF.

Tiny Annie is an amiable blonde with the verve of a 20-year-old starting out in the industry. She talks with clients and colleagues at every opportunity. "It's so rewarding to see all of us from different parts of the world exchanging ideas. I try to promote as much communication as possible between salons and schools," she enthuses. In her quest to make hair colour fun and accessible, and colour and perms co-exist without damaging the hair, she's experimented with everything from paint rollers to cake icers!

She still feels there's room for improvement, however: "There have been significant leaps forward in colour and perming - such as products that both lift and tone - but neither is perfect. We've yet to develop a colour that lasts. Even now, colour fades with general wear and tear, and from exposure to the elements. Protective products reduce fading, but there's still more that needs to be done." I'm very excited about smaller Sassoon studio salons opening in new areas, and the re-built Davies Mews School, which has every teaching aid you could wish for. It's such a state-of-the-art place to learn and grow."

After over 40 years with Vidal Sassoon, Annie's enthusiasm is as fresh as ever. "Vidal's original philosophy is constantly honoured," she explains. "We put our heart and soul into aiming at the highest standards possible. We want hair to look its best while being easy to maintain. "We work in an energetic and creative environment in which everybody from senior management to the newest recruit is encouraged to experiment - an approach that keeps Vidal Sassoon bubbling." That's why Annie's sure she'll be with the organisation until she retires.

The Fellowship of Hair Artists, now known as the Fellowship of British Hairdressing, honoured Annie in 2002 with the Lifetime Achievement Award for her outstanding contribution to the industry. The secret of her success? "Hard work, team work and dedication. Just sit there expecting it to happen, and it won't," she says. Annie deserves every praise for constantly raising standards. She lives in London with her partner John, a classic car rally enthusiast.

Photo: Colin Roy

Tim describes his work as high fashion graphic - extremely simplistic cuts that are true to Vidal's original vision. Over the past decade, he has helped develop all of the Sassoon cutting techniques, including the Bias cut, the Wrap and the A-line fringe. His favourite, however, is Kabuki - a 80s glamorous-punk look adopted by New Romantics everywhere. As a fashion visionary, and a man who creates seasonal Sassoon hair collections Tim is frequently asked for quotes and interviews by editors and broadcast media in many countries. He is a witty, articulate speaker whose presence commands sell-out audiences from Japan to Sweden.

Tim joined Vidal Sassoon in Manchester in 1974 at the age of 15. Commitment and creative vision soon propelled him through the ranks to regional art director, a new role created specially for him. Now international creative director, all of Sassoon's salons, schools and academies throughout Germany, North America and Britain benefit from Tim's artistic flair and long-term creative perspective. The talents of his superior international creative team are in demand around the globe.

"I get a lot of satisfaction seeing the team develop," says Tim. "Standards are improving vastly all the time. It's always a great hair day when our young are so receptive: I feel extremely hopeful for the future of hairdressing in the UK. There's a wealth of originality here. We may not have money, but we British hairdressers lead the way in creativity!"

You can bet your bottom dollar that those watching Tim and Annie at work are inspired to return straight to their salon to try out what they've just seen on clients. That's why they are photographed together - the industry sees them as complementary. The pair speak in a cut and colour language hungrily picked up by student hairdressers, and in turn the high street. I'm sure Vidal is proud. His is a lucky company to have such a vibrant pair to educate the Icons of tomorrow.

AT 50, TIM HARTLEY - LIKE VIDAL, THE LATE ROGER THOMPSON AND HERTA KELLAR BEFORE HIM - IS ONE OF THE FOREMOST HAIRCUTTERS IN THE WORLD. I'M CONSTANTLY IMPRESSED BY THE PRECISION AND FRESHNESS OF HIS WORK WHENEVER I'VE SEE HIM ON STAGE, OR AT THE SASSOON ACADEMY CREATING NEW HAIRCUTS. HOW HE PLANS A NEW CUT MUST BE THE SAME WAY AN ARCHITECT WORKS, ON THE DRAWING BOARD FIRST. I'VE NEVER HEARD HIM MAKE EXCUSES FOR A BAD JOB.

Photos: Colin Roy

JO IS ANOTHER STAR WHO STARTED OUT WITH VIDAL IN THE 60S, BEFORE JOINING DANIEL GALVIN AS A PARTNER IN HIS COLOUR SALON, WHERE SHE BEGAN TO ESTABLISH HER REPUTATION AS "THE BEST TINTER ON THE PLANET" (AMERICAN VOGUE).

TODAY, SHE HAS A MAGNIFICENT SALON SPECIALISING IN COLOUR AND STYLING NEXT DOOR TO THE CONNAUGHT HOTEL, AND OPPOSITE NICKY CLARKE IN THAT GOLDEN MILE OF MAYFAIR. AS JO SAYS: "YEARS AGO, THE BELIEF WAS THAT STYLE CAME FIRST AND COLOUR STAYED FIRMLY IN THE BACKGROUND. IT WAS HIGHLY UNUSUAL FOR A COLOURIST TO SET UP A SALON PUTTING COLOUR IN THE FOREFRONT." ACROSS THE ROAD IS THE JO HANSFORD ACADEMY, MAKING HER THE FIRST FEMALE HAIR COLOURIST TO HAVE HER OWN IN LONDON.

Her popularity stems from her ability to really understand people, listen to what they want and deliver the kind of results that leaves the client feeling on top of the world. From an initial staff of eight, she's built up a close-knit team of all ages and backgrounds who share core values, premised on offering the best service to every-body. People travel from all corners to have their hair coloured by the salon. Two fashionistas in particular have for the last 32 years flown from Australia to London three times a year just to have their hair coloured by Jo's expert hands. "Hair can completely affect the way someone feels about themselves. The ability to transform an individual's image - to give them a new lease of life - is a gift to be cherished", argues Jo.

Her colour skills, like those of Annie Humphries', are so exciting that she'll inevitably stay at the pinnacle of her profession. Befittingly, it is Annie and Vidal that Jo thanks for her wisdom and considerable experience: "It was an honour to work for Vidal, and I'm equally privileged to have had Annie as my mentor - she is a true diva!" Today, Jo is respected in her own right as a creator of wonderful colour stories on a variety of stars such as Elizabeth Hurley, Cate Blanchett and Minnie Driver.

Jo has lots of celebrity stories, such as the time she coloured Richard Burton's hair in his hotel room with her tint bowl resting on the big bump, which bore her daughter (and now PR), Joanna, a few days later! Then there's her secret visits to colour Christine Keeler's hair after the Profumo Affair. And her ongoing work with one of Britain's favourite actors, David Jason. Few hairdressers have had the privilege of working with so many names.

Jo is yet another Brit with an eponymous product line, launched in 1997. Success in these years of hard business on the streets of London is something we have every right to be proud of.

TRAINED BY SASSOON, INSPIRED BY SORBIE
AND ALDO COPPOLA, KEITH HARRIS IS AN IMMENSELY
CHARISMATIC HAIRDRESSER.
BASED IN LOS ANGELES, THE MAN WHO ATTEMPTED
HIS FIRST TENTATIVE HAIR CUT AT 15, NOW JETS AROUND
THE WORLD TRANSFORMING THE HAIR OF MODELS,
FILM STARS AND DUCHESSES.

A darling of the advertising industry, whether working on an ad for Vodaphone or a new look for Ruby Wax, Keith is trusted not only by the stars but by his peers who are constantly inspired by his easy-going manner and strong artistic direction.

Three times winner of the Avant Garde Hairdresser of the Year Award, and a member of the Hall of Fame, his work has been published extensively in the UK and abroad. An innovator of his craft, Keith produces educational videos on tonging, dressing long hair and dry cutting, which are part of the further education curriculum for all new hairdressers in the UK. Major multinational hair companies have faith in his eye for predicting trends.

I hadn't seen Keith for over a year when I went to meet him at the Wella studio in London. He'd lost over three stone (but looked cheekier than ever with that sparkle in his eyes), and I just didn't recognise him, even though I've known him and admired his work for a long time. I've always wondered how he survives not having a salon; he simply travels the world, free as a bird.

He took me on a tour of the city in his black convertible Mercedes before parking by the London Eye on the Thames, where we had a coffee and talked and talked with this monstrous wheel turning slowly and silently behind us. "Well, Harold", he said. "Work here has slowed down: I'm seeking my fortune in the States". London's loss is America's gain.

DANIEL HERSHESON IS AN INFLUENTIAL AND EXCITING STYLIST AT THE FOREFRONT OF QUALITY HAIRDRESSING. WITH LUKE, HE FORMS A RARE FATHER AND SON TEAM RESPONSIBLE FOR CONSISTENTLY FASHIONABLE CUTS AND STYLES.

SOMEWHAT AGAINST HIS FATHER JACK, HIMSELF A HAIRDRESSER, DANIEL ENTERED THE INDUSTRY AT THE AGE OF 15 AS AN APPRENTICE TO XAVIER WENGER, WHERE HE GAINED GOOD, BASIC TRAINING, BEFORE MOVING ON AS AN ASSISTANT AT MICHAELJOHN THREE YEARS LATER.

At 21, he went into partnership with old school friend Neville Tucker to open Neville Daniel in the heart of fashionable London. "Neville Daniel took off straight away. We had queues virtually every day," he recalls. As upmarket and chic as the clients, the salon was designed by Terry Moore and David Callcott (of the then John Michael Design), commissioned specially by Daniel despite the fact that Terry had never before worked on a salon. Terry has since designed the salons of Charles Worthington, and more recently Daniel Galvin. Four salons (including a small one in trichologist Phillip Kingsley's clinic) and even greater success followed, but unfortunately the bubble burst and on 5th July 1990 Daniel left the partnership. "There was a lot of emotion that day," he says.

Today, he is well-established in the top echelons of the market at his eponymous salon on Mayfair's Conduit Street, where clients include Joely Richardson, Liberty Ross and Jennifer Anniston. If I remember rightly, Elizabeth Taylor was a regular when in London.

With son Luke he bridges the gap between salon and session hairdressing, bringing real, fashionable hairstyles to clients. "Our visuals epitomise this," he explains. "The cuts and styles they display are exactly what we do in the salon. Others display photography that has no relevance to their day-to-day work. I've always believed that a woman of 60 and a girl of 16 can have the same fashionable style - it's just about how you adapt it." Daniel is rightly proud of his achievements. "Four years ago we created a bowl-shaped look called the Shunk, which appeared on Chanel's catwalk shows the following season. Recently, we created a new wavy, textured look called Wavy Gravy", he says. "Daniel Hersherson is not about me or Luke as personalities, or the celebrities we work with. We'd much rather people talked about what we do."

After 36 years in the industry, Daniel has seen it all. "Hairdressing is continuously evolving," he says. "It's important to have an open mind about what is acceptable, what is right and the way you work."

LUKE HERSHESON, SON OF FAMOUS FATHER DANIEL, HAS BUILT HIMSELF A PRESTIGIOUS REPUTATION AS A RISING STAR IN HAIRSTYLING.

THE 24-YEAR-OLD HAS WANTED TO BE A HAIRDRESSER, SINCE HE WAS A TODDLER, IN SPITE OF HIS FATHER'S EARLY LACK OF ENTHUSIASM, AND EVEN THOUGH HE SPENT MOST OF HIS FREE TIME WORKING AT NEVILLE DANIEL, THE LONDON SALON HIS FATHER OWNED WITH NEVILLE TUCKER. "I DIDN'T ENCOURAGE HIM AT FIRST BECAUSE I WANTED TO MAKE SURE IT WAS HIS OWN CHOICE, UNTIL AT LEAST HE'D FINISHED SCHOOL," EXPLAINS DANIEL. AT 18, AFTER AN ABORTED SIX-MONTHS AT UNIVERSITY, LUKE OFFICIALLY BEGAN TRAINING WITH DANIEL, SINCE WHEN THE PAIR HAVE BEEN INSEPARABLE.

"We are very much a family partnership; What's good for me is good for Daniel, and vice versa. We're both on the same wavelength," says Luke, who learnt virtually everything he knows from his father. "He's instilled in me the importance of continually learning. Fashion and people constantly evolve, nothing ever stands still, so creativity has to adapt - this is what's so exciting."

In his seven years at Daniel Hersheson, Luke in his various roles has brought vitality to the business. Naturally, he cuts hair in the salon, but as a session hairdresser he spends half his time on shoots, catwalks, television shows and music videos. "I'm also responsible for marketing the salon. When Daniel opened the salon it wasn't rocking the world. It's rewarding to think that 13 years later, we're an internationally-recognised niche brand. As a policy, we don't to go in for hair awards. As a salon we're following a different path to everyone else." Last year, the team launched a successful range of professional styling tools in Selfridges, building on a similar launch five years ago when they were first to introduce professional styling tools for home use. "The range very much came from us - nothing was dealt with by any other company. We travelled the East in search of the best manufacturers and designers," says Luke.

One of the young names that I often read about in international publications, Luke is the choice of major models and pop stars such as Natalie Imbruglia and Kylie, whose hair he has been styling for almost two years. Not that celebrity is important to father or son: "Daniel Hersherson is not about being in every magazine and on every television programme. It's about bringing hairdressing back to what you do, not who you do." Luke would like to continue as he is for the foreseeable future. "I want to keep learning and working at the top level that I am." Daniel has no doubt that the family protégé will succeed: "Extremely hard working, he has vision, a bright business brain, and will achieve what he wants."We have a lot of creative excitement yet to come from Luke, but we must be patient. It takes time to build an iconic reputation.

LIKE MANY IN HIS PROFESSION, MARK STARTED HAIRDRESSING AT 15, WORKING IN A LOCAL SALON IN HIS HOMETOWN OF HULL, ON THE RECOMMENDATION OF A GIRLFRIEND. "I THOUGHT IT WOULD BE A GREAT PLACE TO MEET GIRLS. IT WAS!" HE RECALLS AT 18, HE JOINED THE BRITISH HAIRDRESSING TEAM, TRAVELLING AROUND THE WORLD WINNING GOLD MEDALS FOR HIS COUNTRY. "THE LESSONS AND SKILLS I LEARNT COMPETING ARE AMONGST SOME OF THE MOST VALUABLE OF MY CAREER," HE SAYS.

FOUR YEARS LATER, HE BOUGHT THE HULL SALON HE ORIGINALLY TRAINED IN AND STARTED ENTERING THE BRITISH HAIRDRESSING AWARDS, WINNING THE TITLE OF NORTHERN HAIRDRESSER OF THE YEAR THREE TIMES, WITH MANY MORE AWARDS TO FOLLOW, MOST RECENTLY INTERNATIONAL HAIRDRESSER OF THE YEAR FOR TWO SUCCESSIVE YEARS. THE TALENTS OF THE MARK HILL CREATIVE TEAM WERE RECENTLY RECOGNISED WHEN THEY WERE AWARDED BRITISH ARTISTIC TEAM OF THE YEAR 2003 - THE FIRST NON-LONDON BASED TEAM TO DO SO.

What does Mark do with all his awards? "All the major ones are on show in the salon, some at home, and other's at my dad's house. I'm not the sort to put them at the back of a cupboard as they all represent key moments in my career."

Now a well-known face, over the last six years Mark has appeared on over 250 British television programmes. He recalls the first time he was asked for an autograph: "I was both flattered and embarrassed! I have never aimed to be famous, simply determined to reach the top of my profession."

Mark pinpoints the 1970s and the onset of precision cutting as the start of the rise in the popularity of hairdressers. The media has never been more interested in hair, and so it is only natural to be interested in those who shape the way they look, he argues. "I believe it is essential that the industry continues to build our relationship with the media, and educate the public how integral their hair is to the way they look and feel," he adds.

Mark is often described as a visionary, to which he responds: "I am flattered to think I can influence the way people think about hair. I have two contrasting sides to my work; one is the experimental and progressive side, seeking to develop something edgy and beautiful. The other is making women look irresistibly sexy."

This hair couturier's masterplan is to make Mark Hill an international brand "- like John Frieda. I am only 36, and know that if I work hard, anything is possible," he says.

Although I have known of Mark for a long while, I don't have the pleasure of knowing him. But after our photoshoot I hope it will not be to long before our paths cross again.

2004: Leeds salon opens
2003: British Hairdresser of the Year
       International Hairdresser of the Year
2002: International Hairdresser of the Year
       British Hairdressing Team of the Year
2001: International Hairdresser of the Year
       Mark Hill styling range launched

2000: World Master Award, Australia and New York
       British Hairdresser of the Year
       Hairdresser's Hairdresser of the Year
       Most Outstanding Young Hairdresser of his Generation
1999: Creative Hairdresser of the Year
       Avant Garde Hairdresser of the Year
1998: Creative Hairdresser of the Year
1997: World Master Award, New York
       Avant Garde Hairdresser of the Year
1988: Mark Hill salon opens in Hull

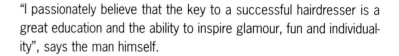

ANDREW IS ONE OF THE MOST INFLUENTIAL AND RESPECTED HAIRDRESSERS IN THE UK. HIS QUIET, RELAXED APPROACH TO HAIRDRESSING HAS HELPED TO CREATE LOOKS FOR INFLUENTIAL MODELS, CELEBRITIES, ACTRESSES AND MUSICIANS INCLUDING SOPHIE ANDERTON, ALANIS MORRISETTE, JODIE KIDD AND SARAH COX.

HIS EXPERIENCE AS AN INNOVATOR AND TREND PREDICTOR HELPS LEADING PRODUCT MANUFACTURERS SUCH AS P&G AND SCHWARZKOPF CREATE ATTRACTIVE IMAGES FOR BOTH THE PUBLIC AND INDUSTRY. SESSIONS WITH REVERED PHOTOGRAPHERS PATRICK DEMARCHELIER AND ELLEN VON UNWORTH, FOR EXAMPLE, STAND OUT IN HIS PHOTOGRAPHY PORTFOLIO.

"I passionately believe that the key to a successful hairdresser is a great education and the ability to inspire glamour, fun and individuality", says the man himself.

The chosen stylist for the international Elite Model Look of the Year, Andrew's career began over 20 years ago when he was stylist, staff trainer and principal of schools and academy at Vidal Sassoon. In the early 90s, he opened his first salon dedicated to styling London's eclectic street scene. The warm and welcoming Andrew Jose Salon - a Vogue Salon of the Year - at 1 Charlotte Street, Fitzroy Square, London followed in 1995.

An active member of the Fellowship of British Hairdressers and Global Ambassador for Schwarzkopf, Andrew promotes British hairdressing talent all over the world. He employs 30 people in a salon and academy in the fairytale city of Prague.

Innovative as he is, Andrew broadcast his Salon 99 hair show live across the world on the Internet. He also promotes British style overseas with the British Government's Department of Trade and Industry, which is surely a good part of the reason why in 1997, his business was recognised as an Investors in People UK* company. Andrew has two young girls, Taylor and Jade, with his long-term partner Charmaine.

The Tate Modern gallery on London's Southbank was the scene of Andrew's Icons photo shoot. As we arrived, a large group of photographers were going in. Luckily, I was wearing my press pass from Vidal's shoot the day before, so we slipped in amongst them. Almost immediately, I saw the first picture I wanted to take - Andrew beneath Rebecca Horn's hanging piano (Concert for Anarchy 1990), something I'd never seen before. Within minutes a security guard came over and said: "You can't take photographs in the gallery." I apologised politely, but I knew I already had it in the bag.

* Investors in People UK is the national standard which sets a level of good practice for the training and development of people to achieve business goals.

Photo: Babar Khan

JASON IS ONE OF MY MOST SUCCESSFUL JUNIORS TO MAKE THE GRADE AND ACHIEVE INTERNATIONAL SUCCESS CREATING SHOWS AND HAIR PHOTOGRAPHY LIKE YOU'VE NEVER SEEN BEFORE.

HOW MANY OF US CAN CLAIM TO HAVE WORKED WITH BARRY LATEGAN, HELMUT NEWTON, SARAH MOON, DAVID MONTGOMERY, NORMAN EALES, BERT STERN, WALTER CHIN, SHIN SUGINO, BABAR KAHN, MYRON ZABOL...?

We met in 1965, when I trained him at my Hampstead salon. Joining me on shoots, he met so many models, photographers, art directors, and so on. I could see that hairdressing had developed into his passion. His first solo shoot was with Charlotte Rampling for SHE, and from then on things started to roll for Jason.

Around 1970 I was due to leave the capital to work as consultant to Seligman & Latz in the US. Jason wanted to join me, so I found him a job with another British superstar, Charles Booth, in his La Coupe salon in Canada, where his very first client was a gorgeous woman. Sitting in his chair, she said: "I want you to shag me".
Jason stared at her.
Cautious, he replied: "Here?"
"Where would you like to do it?" she asked. Still unsure, he leaned closer and wondered if they could do this somewhere else. She looked at him baffled, when her face suddenly changed to wear an unfavourable expression.

A light finally going off in his head, Jason asked the lovely lady if she knew what it meant to shag someone. "To cut my hair of course", came the response. "Well, maybe in the colonies. But not back home where it means to have sex", he explained. With that, she rose from the chair, slapped him across the face and walked out. Three weeks later she was back and he gave her the best shag of her life.

In 1972, Jason opened his own salon, BIBA Hair, before moving to Toronto where he lives with his wife, Areti. He is president of Kearns Davidson Hair & Skin Care, which he founded in 1998. Still a dear friend, I am very proud of Jason's accomplishments.

1998: Founded Kearns Davidson Hair & Skincare
1980: Moved from Montreal to Toronto
1972: Opened BIBA Hair, Montreal
1970: Moved to La Coupe in Montreal, Canada
1964: Began training with Harold Leighton in Hampstead, London

INTERNATIONALLY RENOWNED, GUY KREMER IS A CHARISMATIC BLEND OF GALLIC CHARM AND INNOVATIVE TALENT. AN OUTSTANDING SHOWMAN, HE STUNS AUDIENCES WITH PERFECTLY ENTWINED CHIGNONS, COMPLEMENTING DESIGNER DRESSES FROM THE CREAM OF THE FASHION WORLD. HIS WORK FOR CELEBRITY DESIGNERS, ISABELL KRISTENSEN AND MARIA GRACHVOGEL, BRINGS HIS ELEGANCE AND STYLE TO CATWALK AND CHARITY SHOW AUDIENCES AROUND THE WORLD.

VOTED ONE OF THE TOP 75 EDUCATORS OF THE CENTURY BY USA INDUSTRY BIBLE, MODERN SALON, THE INTERNATIONAL STYLE-MAKER IS IN CONSTANT DEMAND AT SEMINARS WORLDWIDE. THANKS TO HIS FLAIR FOR COMBINING THE CLASSIC WITH THE FUNKY, TO CREATE STYLES THAT TRANSFORM HAIR, LEADING UK COMPANIES REGULARLY BOOK HIM TO GUEST STAR IN EUROPEAN SEMINARS.

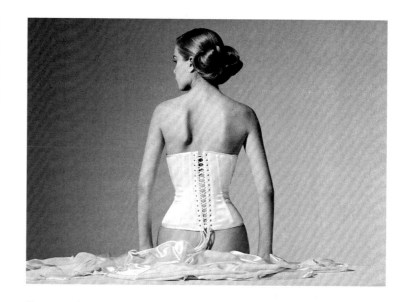

Guy travels so much it's hard to keep up with him. When we met, he'd just returned from a retrospective of Jean Paul Gaultier's flamboyant creations at the Victoria & Albert Museum. What an honour and achievement for Guy to be asked to participate in the show. He was exhausted, but full of smiles and ready for the camera. Much as Guy loves the glamour of the international jet set - celebrity clients include the Duchess of York and Shirley Bassey - he's happiest when he's working at his salon, where everyone is a VIP. "I believe women should show their femininity to the full," he says.

Born in Talange, France in 1952, Guy came to England as a 22-year-old stylist with Winchester-based Hans of Vienna. In 1977, he opened his own salon in the same town, where he works to this day, charging a modest £56 for a cut and blow. Of course, this means a wait of several months for an appointment with the man himself, but his loyal clients understand that great cuts come to those with patience.

Guy's reputation is built on a foundation of commitment technique and genuine flair. Why else would a man with a single salon, in an English county town, be in such demand worldwide?

UK AWARDS
2001: L'Oreal Colour Trophy
1997: Fellowship Hairdresser of the Year
L'Oreal Men's Image Award
1995: L'Oreal Colour Trophy
1993: British Men's Hairdresser of the Year
1991: British Hairdressing Hall of Fame

INTERNATIONAL AWARDS
2000: Best Men's Collection AIPP 2000 Grand Trophy
of the Professional Press
1997: Voted one of Top 75 Educators of the Century
by Modern Salon magazine
1993: Sup'hair Trophee Angleterre

IN THE COURSE OF AN ILLUSTRIOUS CAREER, LEONARD LEWIS ACHIEVED FAME AS ONE OF THE MOST EXPRESSIVE HAIRDRESSERS IN THE UK. A TRUE ORIGINAL, HE WAS CHARISMATIC ENOUGH TO NATURALLY BEFRIEND MANY OF HIS CELEBRITY CLIENTS.

LEONARD' STARTED HIS REMARKABLE CAREER WAS ON AN APPRENTICESHIP WITH THE LATE ROSE EVANSKY, BEFORE PURSUING FURTHER TOP-NOTCH TRAINING WITH VIDAL SASSOON IN THE 1960S.

Once he'd graduated as a top stylist, the young Leonard opened his own salon - Leonard & Raphael - at 34 Duke Street, which was such a success that they moved to a huge house on Upper Grosvenor Street near the American Embassy. When Raphael lost interest in the business, the minimalist salon became known simply as Leonard. Covering five floors and housing a hundred staff, it was a vast creative machine producing some of the most glamorous haircuts and colour in the country. I would often drop by to catch up on the latest happenings.

Leonard attended to some of the wealthiest names of the day. His favourite celebrity? "Well it's hard to say, there were so many," he answers, but Twiggy and Tony Curtis come to mind. He particularly chose to work in film, most famously cutting and styling the hair of the main actors in Stanley Kubrick's A Clockwork Orange, 2001, Barry Lyndon, The Shining and Full Metal Jacket. "If you understood what Stanley was doing, you had no problems with him," says Leonard. Everyone knew Leonard by his hands, which always seemed to be holding a comb and scissors. As I recall they were insured for £1,000,000, or as Leonard puts it, "a hell of a lot." Not that he has ideas above his station. "Some of us tend to forget that at the end of the day we are public servants," he says.

Like his teacher Vidal, Leonard trained many of today's leading hairdressers including Daniel Galvin, John Frieda and Nicky Clarke. "He was a genius; his work was ahead of its time. To this day many of London's top stylists owe a debt of gratitude we can never fully repay," says Nicky. These guys got London's hair scene swinging! Not that Leonard's completely happy with the industry as it stands. "Anyone can open a salon and claim to be a hairdresser, to the detriment of good practitioners. That's wrong. The government should make Hair Council registration mandatory."

Sadly, Leonard has not been a well man since suffering a brain tumour 14 years ago. The 65-year-old misses his salon and his art; but we miss him more.

FROM HIS BEGINNING AS A HAIRDRESSER IN LONDON,
TO HIS CURRENT REIGN AS VICE PRESIDENT OF CREATIVE FOR
SEBASTIAN INTERNATIONAL, ROBERT LOBETTA LIVES BY THE
MANTRA: "A MAN IN MOTION STAYS IN MOTION."
SCULPTOR, PAINTER, PHOTOGRAPHER, HAIRDRESSER -
HE IS A RENAISSANCE MAN.

As a young man, Robert was Ricci Burns' stylist and art director, creating provocative avant-garde hair designs, which eventually became his signature. At the end of the 70s, he redefined the image of Michaeljohn for Michael Rasser and John Isaacs through innovative hair designs, such as The Twist and The Weave.

From the small screen to the big screen, Robert's talents preceded him. In 1985, acclaimed American film director Ridley Scott asked him to create and design hair sculptures for the film Legend. Ironically, in the same year that the British Hairdressing Awards named him Avant Garde Hairdresser of the Year, he gave up hairdressing to work in the field of total imaging, putting to use all he'd learned from working with so many talented people. Beauty companies were desperately searching in the early 80s for brand imaging that would differentiate their products from the pack. Robert's reputation for outrageous hair designs pushed him to the forefront of print and television advertising, where he caught the attention of Geri Cusenza of Sebastian. Their creative relationship lasted until her departure in 1997, when Robert became the company's full-time creative director.

In 2000, The Fellowship for British Hairdressing recognised Robert's creative genius by presenting him with the Fellowship Special Fashion Award - a testimony to his creative influence in the UK and worldwide beauty industry. The North American Hair Association recently honoured him with the coveted Lifetime Achievement Award. "My work is an evolving abstract process. I'm driven by a desire for perfection: you are only as good as your last piece of work," he explains.

With such a formidable reputation, I was rather scared when I met Robert at a restaurant on the Thames, where he was eating with his good friend, Anthony Mascolo. Some vodka and lager helped kill the nerves, and as soon as our meal was over, we walked to Albert Bridge. "If I sit on the bollard and you shoot from there, we should be OK," he directed. When Robert speaks, you listen.

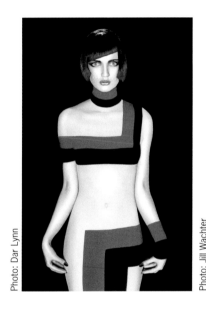

Photo: Dar Lynn

Photo: Jill Wachter

HAIRDRESSER, AUTHOR, PRESENTER, EDUCATOR, INNOVATOR AND MOTIVATIONAL SPEAKER, VIVIENNE MACKINDER IS A REMARKABLY ACCOMPLISHED WOMAN.

SHE GREW UP IN LONDON WHERE, AS ARTISTIC DIRECTOR FOR GRANDMASTERS VIDAL SASSOON AND TREVOR SORBIE, SHE DEVELOPED AN EXPERTISE IN PRECISION CUTTING AND AN EYE FOR ORIGINAL DESIGN. IN 1991, SHE SPREAD HER WINGS AND WENT TO AMERICA WHERE SHE SOON BEGAN TO WIN AWARDS, NORTH AMERICAN HAIRDRESSING AWARD FOUR TIMES AND THE EDITORS CHOICE AWARDS THREE TIMES.
BY 1994, SHE WAS MATRIX ESSENTIALS' INTERNATIONAL ARTISTIC DIRECTOR, WORKING ON EDITORIAL AND ADVERTISING, FASHION SHOWS AND PRODUCT DEVELOPMENT.

Vivienne is the founder of the popular Roots and Wings retreats, the author of several internationally published books, and with director Aldo Belkouar recently produced an industry first - the documentary *I'm Not Just a Hairdresser* - a seminal film, if it teaches the public to appreciate what the individuals in our industry do to create new stories and new looks. One day hairdressers will get closer to Oscar nominations.

Vivienne's passion for performing has been with her since childhood: "I was on stage at the age of six and have never left, although my performance has changed from dance to doing hair. For the past decade, in addition to being a featured guest artist in major shows and events, I have presented my one-woman show to thousands around the world," she says.

With artist Oscar Bond, whom she met during her Sassoon days, Vivienne set up the Mackinder-Bond Academy providing the real-world setting of a working New York Salon, in which they co-host a series of educational short programmes.

"My experience has taught me that the key to success is ongoing education," she says. "In all creative educational endeavors, a balance must exist between teaching the fundamentals and encouraging freedom of expression. You must learn the rules before you break them."

Looking ahead, she adds: "As fashion designers look back with romantic nostalgia reinventing trends from the 1920s to 1980s, I see the future showcasing a new type of glamour, a return to style and feminine spirit, best defined by soft, full textured hair."

Much has happened since vibrant Vivienne and I first met over 10 years ago. She's climbed the heights of US hairdressing and is looking better than ever; the heavy work load and travel obviously agree with her.

One-time Student Hairdresser of Great Britain, Martyn opened his first salon in Knightsbridge in 1991 at the age of 31. He opened a second at the prestigious Harbour Club in Chelsea in 1994. Within three years, he'd achieved his long-held ambition of moving his main salon to Mayfair - commonly considered a major stepping stone to greater success.

Five years later, he added a complete extra floor - probably to make room for all his celebrity clients such as Sophie Dahl, Elle McPherson and Naomi Campbell. The most prominent in his memory is Melanie Griffith; he recalls doing her hair at the Ritz when she was just 17, and not yet a household name. The Hollywood actress was accompanying her mum, Tippi Hedren, to the premier of Roar. Today, Martyn owns a further two salons in Mayfair.

In his 13 years in hairdressing Martyn has done countless interviews, step-by-step guides, worked for all the major magazines and newspapers, made many radio TV appearances and won several awards. He also has an interest in the products aspect of the industry, becoming a consultant to Boots in 1994, and subsequently to Procter and Gamble.

MARTYN STARTED HAIRDRESSING IN 1977, WITH AN APPRENTICESHIP IN RUGBY, WARWICKSHIRE, AFTER WHICH HE ACQUIRED A CITY & GUILDS CERTIFICATE IN LADIES AND GENTS HAIRDRESSING AND WIGMAKING, AND AN ADVANCED CITY & GUILDS IN HAIRDRESSING.

IT WAS DURING HIS 10 YEARS AT MICHAELJOHN THAT MARTYN GREW TO ENJOY WORKING WITH LONG HAIR. HE TAUGHT LONG HAIRDRESSING FOR L'OREAL AND DEVELOPED THEIR FIRST SPECIALIST BRIDAL HAIRDRESSING COURSE. THESE DAYS, MARTYN TEACHES FOR WELLA AS PART OF THEIR BEST OF BRITISH LONG HAIRDRESSING SERIES IN LONDON AND MANCHESTER.

Involvement in hair-care brands led to the launch, in 2002, of his own haircare range for Marks & Spencer - hairdressing history in the making. This was the first time M&S stocked a brand other than their own - MM remains the only own-label sold in the 300 UK stores, and is distributed in most overseas branches including Spain, Dubai, Jersey, Singapore, Hong Kong and Saudi Arabia.

Martyn's favourite London landmark is the Thames. For his photo shoot we wandered from the roof of St Paul's Cathedral to Tower Bridge, and chanced upon this massive bronze Shire horse statue. Thanks to Martyn's high fitness levels he managed to climb on top of it and snap! snap! snap!, we had a ball without collecting a single parking ticket.

WITH A CAREER SPANNING THREE DECADES, SAM MCKNIGHT REMAINS FIRMLY AT THE FOREFRONT OF SESSION HAIRSTYLING. SINCE WORKING ON HIS FIRST VOGUE SHOOT IN 1978, HE HAS COLLABORATED ON HUNDREDS OF THE FASHION BIBLE'S COVERS AND STORIES, WORKING CLOSELY WITH PIONEERING PHOTOGRAPHERS SUCH AS BRUCE WEBER, STEVEN MEISEL, PATRICK DEMARCHELIER, IRVING PENN AND RICHARD AVEDON.

Sam was responsible for many of the unforgettable looks that shaped the fashion and supermodel explosion of the mid-80s. Today's catwalk queens, such as Naomi Campbell, Gisele Bundchen and Kate Moss, continue to have their hair styled by the maestro. His celebrity list has included Nicole Kidman, Cate Blanchett, Kylie Minogue, Madonna, Elizabeth Hurley and Uma Thurman. The most famous, however, was the late Princess Diana whose hair he styled for her most memorable images, up to 1997 - the year of her untimely death.

Sam consistently works with the designers of the moment, such as Giorgio Armani, Prada, Gucci, Chloe, Stella McCartney, Julien MacDonald and Matthew Williamson. In the 90s, he created Vivienne Westwood's exciting catwalk hairstyles. Respected by designers, photographers and journalists worldwide, Sam has kept his place as *the* number one session hairdresser.

His countless professional awards include British Session Hairdresser of the Year for three years running, the coveted Venus award in Paris and New York, and more recently Best Session Hairdresser of the Year at the UK Elle Style Awards 2002.

July 29th 2003 was yet another wonderful experience, meeting Sam at his agency in London's Westbourne Grove. By the time I arrived, he was already on location for a Vogue shoot. As the cab drove up to the scene I could see Sam working his fingers through a model's hair; a beautiful creature, even from a distance.
Sam said: "I'm working with Sophie Dahl. Should I ask her if she'd mind being in the shots? "
You can guess my reply. Wow, she's a corker! No wonder she's such a successful model. My two year wait to shoot Sam was worth it.

Photo: Robert Lobetta

Photo: Clive Arrowsmith

SCOTLAND HAS BRED SOME FINE HAIRDRESSERS IN ITS TIME - PAUL MITCHELL, JENNIFER CHEYNE, IRVINE RUSK, BRIAN DRUM AND TAYLOR FERGUSON TO NAME A FEW. CURRENTLY RULING THE ROOST IN EDINBURGH ARE CHARLIE, JASON AND INDIA MILLER.

CHARLIE OPENED HIS FIRST SOLO SHOP AT THE AGE OF 20. TODAY HE IS THE DRIVING FORCE BEHIND THE SUCCESSFUL CHARLIE MILLER GROUP, RUN WITH HIS WIFE JANET, THEIR SONS JASON AND JOSHUA, DAUGHTER-IN-LAW INDIA, IAN BLYTH AND TERRI ROBERTSON-KIRKWOOD.

In 1976, he was one of four compatriots in a legendary line-up called The Super Scots at Salon International, putting Scotland firmly on the hairdressing map. A founder member of the British Hairdressing Hall of Fame, amongst other awards Charlie has won Scottish Hairdresser of the Year three times.

The Charlie Miller artistic team is today spearheaded by Jason and India. A dynamic husband and wife team, they entered the business in their teens, and as creative and artistic directors enjoy a reputation for introducing innovative concepts such as the Crochet. Their original, often stunning, photographic collections are published worldwide.

At the 2003 MTV Europe Video Music Awards, held in Edinburgh for the first time, the Millers were invited to work their magic on the stars. "Having such a high-profile event with its 6,000-strong audience on our home turf was very special," says Jason. "Whilst most of the stars had a personal hairdresser, India and I were based in the VIP room, where her signature Stitch was requested by the show's two main presenters. Working all day and night between us, our team of eight did about 120 heads, including Minnie Driver's. The next day it was back to business, exhausted but all the better for the experience. "

Leaders in their field, Jason and India carry the flag for the UK hairdressing industry in delivering motivational seminars and workshops (predominantly for L'Oréal Professionnel) to delighted audiences worldwide, from Europe to South Africa. Both formerly British Newcomer of the Year, in 2002 they were the only British hairdressers to collect an award at the Association Internationale Presse Professionnelle Coiffure. Now in their 30s, Jason and India have proudly joined Charlie in the Hall of Fame.

Since hanging up his scissors at the end of 1998, Charlie has concentrated on the company's marketing, PR and business development. The day I photographed the talented trio was Charlie's birthday. Amongst his first words to me were: "I'm 59 and going strong."

Photo: Mark Flisher

DURING THE 1970S HAIRDRESSING WAS VERY MUCH A MAN'S WORLD. APART FROM THE CHARISMATIC CARITA SISTERS, ROSE AND MARIA, IN PARIS AND OUR OWN ROSE EVANSKY IN LONDON, THERE WERE PRECIOUS FEW ORIGINAL FEMALE ACTS ON THE SCENE. CHRISTINE, HOWEVER, IS ONE OF THE FIRST WOMEN, AFTER ROSE, TO SHINE THROUGH IN THE PHOTOGRAPHIC AND ADVERTISING HAIR WORLD.

A STRING OF TALENTED WOMEN FOLLOW IN HER WAKE - RITA RUSK, PAULEEN BEARD, JO HANSFORD, JENNIFER CHEYNE, ANTOINETTE BEENDERS, LISA SHEPERD, SACHA MASCOLO, INDIA MILLER, BEVERLY COBELLA...

Abandoning thoughts of university in the early 60s, Christine started an apprenticeship with Alan Harding, holder of the Rose Bowl and president of the National Hairdressing Federation, on London's Berkeley Square. After a mere 18 months, she was put on the floor to do her first photography work - a makeover for a spring hairstyles edition of Woman.

Pastures new took the form of Maurice and John French's salon on Grosvenor Square, a hive of pop and media people, one of whom - Raymond Oliver - was to become her partner. In 1971 their newly-opened first Mane Line salon in the West End was an immediate hit amongst the music, fashion and advertising industries. Christine's hobby started earning her an extra income when she was employed as a freelance advertising copywriter. This led, in 1974, to her becoming the first hairdresser to be given a write-up in the exclusive pages of the New Yorker magazine. In January the following year comedian Marty Allen took her backstage at the Hilton Las Vegas to meet her idol, Elvis Presley. "It was the most wonderful thing I've done in my whole life. I don't think I spoke for two days afterwards!" she recalls.

The mid-80s saw her adding make-up to her repertoire, and working on commercials such as the award-winning Levi jeans adverts, as well as music videos and movies. She cut and coloured Miranda Richardson and Willem Dafoe's hair for the award-winning Tom and Viv. But the pinnacle of blonde-bobbed Christine's career came in 1992, when she was one of only five hairdressers included in a Victoria & Albert Museum exhibition called Hair. Her contributions were Mane Line photographs, for which she'd done the hair and make-up, small oblong carrier bags designed by Raymond, and customised ashtrays created by both Raymond and Christine themselves. Today, they can be viewed by appointment.

Christine continues to enjoy commissions for commercials and movies. The BBC and film companies regularly send their artists for makeovers at her W1 'shop'. "I'm very visual", she says. "I don't just see hair, I see the whole picture".

PAUL FIRST INTRODUCED HIMSELF TO ME AT ROMAINE'S ON EDGWARE ROAD IN 1952. I WAS 20, HE WAS 17 AND ALREADY A MAN OF MANY TALENTS: A STUDENT AT THE MORRIS SCHOOL OF HAIRDRESSING, SLIM, GOOD-LOOKING, AND WITH A SCOTTISH ACCENT SO BEAUTIFUL THAT YOU NEVER WANTED HIM TO STOP TALKING. SHARING MANY INTERESTS - NOT LEAST SUCCESS - WE SOON FORMED A STRONG FRIENDSHIP THAT WOULD LAST 33 YEARS.

The pictures on page 113 are the work of Richard Avedon:
Paul donning his hat to say goodbye to the world.
This royal ballet dancer was my client, photographed by Eamonn McCabe.
The solar car was shot in Australia by an unknown photographer circa 1988.

Paul and I were addicted to the buzz of competitions. There was one contest for which he couldn't find the right model, so he asked if he could borrow mine, Jean, whom I'd chatted up at a bus stop (models were difficult to come by in those days). Of course, I said yes to my mate. I was enjoying great success with her and hoped it would rub off on him. The next I heard they were living together and I soon found another fabulous face in raven-headed Sylvia, and together we made non-blonde models as fashionable as blondes.

A few years later Paul was working with my other dear friend Vidal, carving out a niche for himself in Britain's number one salon on London's Bond Street. When he'd made his mark, he caught The Queen Elizabeth from Southampton to New York, where he teamed up with Henri Bendel to open his first salon re-creating the London look. That was the last I saw of Paul until he turned up to see me one day at Harrods with the beautiful, blonde Jeanne Braa on his arm. He was in London to do a KMS hair show at the American Embassy, his first in what was at least a 10-year break from The Big Smoke. From then on, whenever he was back in town his first port of call from Heathrow was Harrods.

One year I arranged to meet him after work at his hotel to look at a set of new photos. With him was another beautiful blonde, wearing nothing but skimpy knickers and a tiny T-shirt. Jolina eventually became his wife and the mother of his only son, Angus.

In 1980, with John Paul De Joria, Paul launched the Paul Mitchell professional haircare system in America. Unlike anything else on the market, it changed the way hairdressers work; it helped us be more creative. Near burn-out, he sold his salon group and sailed the seas to make a home in Honolulu. His mum, Jenny, told me he couldn't afford a house and made do with a caravan, I seem to recall. But each time we spoke he'd enthuse about his Awaphuii farmhouse on Pauulio. The stories grew and grew, as did his business and bank balance.

Photo: Eamon Mc Cake

Back in the UK, nobody had heard of Paul Mitchell. In 1986, Maxine and I launched the brand in Britain and sought to change that. Paul gave me his full authority to arrange his promotional photo shoots with my photographer friends Vic Sing, Kim Knott, Russ Malkin and Christophe Kutner. He'd come to London, do the hair and vanish 'til the next time.

With our help, Paul transformed his US style into a sophisticated London look. Together, Roz Rubenstein, Paul's LA-based friend and PR, and I told the world's media. They loved it. And Paul Mitchell became a household name, not just in America, but Europe too. Today, John Paul Mitchell Systems has annual retail sales of approximately $600 million. I'm proud to be part of this success story.

Paul was the most honourable and trusting man I knew, a loyal friend and a great business partner. The one and only time he let us down was when he died. The last time I saw him was when I took Jenny to Mount Sinai Hospital in Los Angeles on 21st April 1989, a few hours before he passed away. As she walked in to see him, he blinked to acknowledge her presence. Surrounded by his son, mum, ex-wives and mistresses, fiancée Milly Kaiserman and close friends, he flew. Destroyed by cancer, he was far too young to leave us.

The funeral took place at a beautiful chapel outside, in which a flock of flamingos rested in a lake. Together, John Paul and I stood next to a larger than life picture of Paul and spoke to hundreds of his people, many of us sobbing. But the first part of his send-off was upbeat; Paul would have liked that.

Soon after the ceremony, around twelve friends, along with Angus, Milly, Jenny, Jeanne, Roz and I, flew to Hawaii. At about 25,000 feet up I was sitting alone, reminiscing, when there was a banging on the window. I thought we'd hit something! Once I'd composed myself I went over to JP to tell him what had just happened. He replied: "It was Paul. Come over here", and with that he went to the luggage rack, opened it and gave me Paul's ashes - an experience I will never forget. We buried him the next day during one of the heaviest downpours of the year on his Awaphuii farm.

DESMOND HAS MANIFESTED HIMSELF AS ONE OF THE MOST VERSATILE AND ARTISTICALLY ACCOMPLISHED HAIRSTYLISTS IN THE UK, BECOMING A SOUGHT-AFTER EDUCATOR WHO CONDUCTS SEMINARS ALL OVER EUROPE AND AMERICA.

HE STARTED LEARNING THE BASICS OF HIS TRADE 24 YEARS AGO IN WOLVERHAMPTON, WEST MIDLANDS IN ENGLAND. ENTERING HAIR COMPETITIONS, DESMOND DISCOVERED THAT HE HAD A NATURAL TALENT AND A DESIRE TO EXCEL. SELIGMAN & LATZ*, OWNERS OF SALONS WORLDWIDE, SOON SNAPPED HIM UP AS PART OF THEIR ARTISTIC TEAM TO STAGE SEMINARS, SHOWS AND PHOTO SESSIONS.

Two years later, he moved to Vidal Sassoon to a more advanced level of styling and dressing hair. At about the same time, he acquired the art of fashion photography. His now award-winning photos are as magnificent as his hairdressing. Desmond's advice to those who want to achieve this kind of success? "Education is the key to life."

Desmond and I go back to the 1980s when I trained him as one of ten new stars that made my Headliners team at Harrods - my London base. Superstar showman Desmond stood out from the crowd from the start; carving out the most amazing shapes, he taught me all about black hair. I still have the fantastic pictures we did together, and I can't believe he was creating such visionary designs way back then.

To me, Desmond and Michael McKenzie epitomised the best of Afro hair artists. Never had I experienced hair cutting the way these two did it. Watching them at work made me wild with joy.

Desmond stuck the course, and went on to prove himself as the exceptionally versatile and artistically accomplished hairstylist he is. With countless number of television appearances to his name, and a huge celebrity clientele, he is currently working in a West End salon three days a week, allowing him time to do catwalk shows, pop videos, magazine shoots... A true gent, he is three times winner of British Hairdressing Awards' Afro Hairdresser of the Year.

* Then known as Essanelle

Photo: Chris Dunlop

Photo: Kevin Macintosh

2003: Opens salon in London
2002: Afro Hairdresser of the Year
2001: Afro Hairdresser of the Year
2000: Black Hair and Beauty/Hall of Fame
1998: Afro Hairdresser of the Year
      Black Hair and Beauty/Wahl Stylist of the Year

1997: Black Hair and Beauty/Wahl Stylist of the Year
      Black Hair and Beauty/Wahl Avant Garde Stylist of the Year
1995: Afro Hair and Beauty Photographic Award
1987: L'Oreal Photo Fashion Gold Award
1984: L'Oreal Colour Trophy Award
1983: TCB Hair and Fashion Award

Photo: Kevin Macintosh

Photo: Kevin Macintosh

Celebrity clients: Julia Roberts, Elle Macpherson, Destiny's Child, Frank Bruno, Denise Lewis, Beverly Knight, Jocelyn Brown
Magazines: Arena, Sunday Telegraph magazine, DJ, Marie Claire, Estetica, Hairdressers Journal, 19, Daily Mail, Esquire

ALTHOUGH GORDON HAS LIVED IN THE UNITED STATES FOR MANY YEARS, HE ENTERED THE PROFESSION IN LONDON IN 1967 AS AN APPRENTICE TO VIDAL. FROM THE AGE OF NINETEEN, HIS WORK APPEARED REGULARLY IN WELL-KNOWN PUBLICATIONS, INCLUDING VOGUE, HARPER'S BAZAAR AND ELLE.

AT 25 HE WAS A PARTNER AND CREATIVE DIRECTOR AT JOSHUA GALVIN, ONE OF LONDON'S MOST DISTINGUISHED SCHOOLS FOR HAIRSTYLING.

He later relocated to the US and in 1977, joined the Regis Corporation as an artistic director, where he helped establish the artistic team and technical programme. Now he's senior vice -president of fashion, education and marketing, and the international creative director in charge of 150 artistic directors internationally. His creativity and talent continuously raises the level of excellence for the company's 45,000 associates worldwide. A true figurehead, the industry looks up to him as a prime educator and designer. No wonder, if reincarnated, he'd like to come back as himself!

Icons shoot Plan A was to photograph him on the Station Isle ferry, sailing around the Statue of Liberty. I woke up in my friend's New Jersey home the day of the shoot to a March morning, thick with, fog, rain and snow. When a car came to collect me, the driver informed me of Plan B - I would meet Gordon at his hotel in central NYC.

Discussing what we should do to capture the city, Damian, Gordon's son, decided that we should go to Brooklyn Bridge and shoot from the lower level. It might sound easy, but not so. The city was on high security and the bridges were manned by the police. After a little English-accented persuasion, they allowed us to take our shots.

Thank the saints Gordon was wearing his best Gieves & Hawkes suit from London's Saville Row, because by this time it was raining and the mist was all around. Well, we all got soaked, but it was worth it: the picture has a kind of magic.

Greeting me at his fine looking salon he went on to introduce me to his staff saying: "This is my dad!", despite the fact that all we have in common is our hairstyle (well, almost!) What a character. With his pierced lip ring and well-defined haircut, he certainly stands out in a crowd.

Adee took me to his flat for our shoot. Rachel, his model of 6'2" her in high heels, and mother came too. My brief was: "I need skin pictures. Something risky." Boy, did he oblige!

I knew this energetic Irish lad was going to be different to the other hairdressers I'd photographed. And I was right. He is the wild cat of the industry, Mr Scissorhands to the stars. We need individuals like this. Reading and seeing his global press coverage on Beckham's Mohican alone is enough to make what hair I have stand on end. As does his extraordinary entry into the industry - a story stranger than fiction - about a painter and decorator who became a hairdresser.

HAVING HEARD ABOUT ADEE AS THE MAN WHO CREATED THE DAVID BECKHAM* HAIRCUTS, I DROVE TO OUR FIRST MEETING ON THE ESSEX COAST WITH A LITTLE TREPIDATION.

ADEE'S DIRECTIONS WERE JUST "LEIGH-ON-SEA" BUT FINDING HIS SALON WAS EASY. "ASK ANYBODY IN THE STREET AND THEY'LL DIRECT YOU," I WAS TOLD. HE WAS RIGHT. I ASKED THREE PEOPLE: THEY ALL KNEW STRANGEWAYS.

In 1991 Adee, who is originally from Kilkenny, found himself in Essex where he befriended Lee Stafford through one of his stylists, Martyn Holmes. Specialising in painting effects at the time, Lee employed Adee to paint his new salon in Leigh-on-Sea. Immersed in salon life, Adee began to take a serious interest in hairdressing. Training with Lee by day, by night, he soon started hitting hairdressing headlines himself. Now the British Men's Hairdresser of the Year 2000 is haircutter to Liza Minelli and the Sultan of Brunei and gets tipped £2,500. Don't be surprised to find yourself reading the book and watching the movie one day.

2001: Stylist of the Year
2000: British Men's Hairdresser of the Year
        Retailer of the Year

*Those initials DB - they ring a bell from my days when they stood for the David Bowie, or better still the haircut I did for the Daily Express in 1967 - Ducks Behind.

CHRISTOPHER IS SO COOL, SO LAID BACK, AND SUCH
A NICE MAN. THE CHESHIRE-BORN BARBER AND HAIRSTYLIST
HAS BEEN PERFECTING HIS ART FOR OVER 40 YEARS, EVER
SINCE HE STARTED CYCLING 10 MILES EVERY MORNING TO
A LADIES HAIRDRESSING SALON IN DERBYSHIRE, IN FACT.
LIKE A GOOD WINE, HE IMPROVES WITH AGE.

As part of the first Sassoon team to go to the United States, Christopher opened Vidal's first ladies hair salon in New York City in 1965, when he was just 22. After leaving the organisation in 1973, he travelled the country with our friend Paul Mitchell, appearing in educational shows for major product manufacturers, such as the permanent wave company, Rilling.

1978 was a busy year for Christopher - he married his "perfect woman" Susan, and opened his own salon in the elegant Gramercy area of New York, training staff in the fine art of individual styling, always with the highest standards of customer service. Since 2000, he, along with his dynamic team of four, has been cutting hair in his wonderful studio in Red Bank, Central New Jersey, a quaint little town about 90 minutes from New York. It's the type of place where the buzz hits you the second you walk through the doors.

He invited me back to his new home, minutes away from the studio, when the March snow was thick on the ground. It was cold, that's for sure. As you can see, the house he shares with Susan and their teenage daughters Devon Elizabeth and Kaitlin Jane, enjoys a spectacular setting on the banks of Shadow Lake, Two River.

Christopher has found a way of combining his two loves of gardening and haircutting: he and Susan are currently working on customised flower essences for his clients. Integrating his inner and outer self has become increasingly important to Christopher, since he began practising yoga two years ago. "Learning something new challenges and inspires me to keep my haircutting fresh", he says. Life is good.

RAMSEY IS ANOTHER STAR PUPIL WHO WORKED WITH ME IN THE HARRODS HAIR AND BEAUTY SALON, DURING THE EARLY 70S, AND HAS GONE ON TO MAKE WAVES AROUND THE WORLD. WE'VE HAD SOME FINE TIMES TOGETHER, ESPECIALLY WHEN HE ASSISTED ME ON TOUR ACROSS THE US FOR FABERGÉ, UNDER THE DIRECTION OF MILTON BARRIE; AND WHEN LUIS LLONGUERAS, ONE OF THE WORLD'S MOST RENOWNED HAIRDRESSERS, INVITED US TO BARCELONA IN 1976 TO WORK AT HIS MAJOR EXPO.

In 1980, armed with a few thousand dollars, Ramsey moved to Tinsel Town, where he put to the test his obvious talent as a session and showbiz hairdresser. With the help of Sex and the City siren, Kim Cattrall, and Nick Marcelino, head of the Universal Studios make-up department, Ramsey's dream has come true - he's made it from Harrods to Hollywood.

"I met Nick through a mutual friend," explains Ramsey. "He'd taken a shine to me whilst I was showing the Universal staff hairdressers how to blow-dry. Kim wanted this look for Tribute, a comedy drama she was starring in; so did Nick. Through some skilful and ethical manoevring he hired me for the movie, which I stayed working on until it was completed, thanks to a continuity clause. This was it, or so I thought."

The first thing Ramsey did was resign from his LA salon and look around for his next gig. "Nothing came my way because I had no seniority and wasn't in the Hollywood Make-up and Hairstylists Union," he recalls. Then disaster struck - the scriptwriters went on strike, forcing him to bartend at night and work the graveyard shift at a blood bank. "My wife Sharon and I worked so hard to pay the bills. We had enough money for one more mortgage payment when I finally got a call from Nick. He'd had to wait until the roster had depleted before he could hire me," he says. Talk about being in the right place at the right time.

At the time there were no male union members, yet all the make-up artists were men. As a male, English hairdresser, Ramsey was rather resented. But he joined later in 1980 and has never looked back.

Some 25 years on, Ramsey has coiffed the hair of most of the era's superstars, such as Tom Cruise and Meg Ryan on Top Gun, Robert de Niro, Mel Gibson, Julia Roberts, Kiefer Sutherland, Mick Jagger, Uma Therman, Charlize Theron, Geoffrey Rush, and Demi Moore and Rob Lowe on St Elmo's Fire.

As I write this, he is flying to Calgary for four weeks to finish a movie called The Lazarus Child with his hero, Andy Garcia. During their 15 years of friendship, Ramsey has worked on all but two of Garcia's films. "In all that time, I have never heard him say a negative thing about anyone. Honourable and principled, he's taught me a great deal," he says of the actor.

Perhaps most impressive of all, Ramsey is the first British hairdresser to win an Emmy Award (that's his baby he's clutching in the diving board shot), for Second Serve, starring his friends Vanessa Redgrave, Diane Keaton and Ellen Barkin. He's also the first British hairdresser to join the American Academy of Motion Picture Arts and Sciences.

Photo: Barry Lategan

HAVING TRAINED WITH LEONARD IN LONDON, AND REGULARLY
WORKED WITH HOLLYWOOD LEGENDS SUCH AS JUDY GARLAND
IN NEW YORK, MICHAEL HAD ALREADY ESTABLISHED AN
ADMIRABLE REPUTATION BEFORE OPENING MICHAELJOHN IN
LONDON WITH JOHN ISAACS IN DECEMBER 1967.

The beau monde demand for the pair's services became so great
that by 1978, they'd opened a salon on Camden Hill Drive in
Beverly Hills. Married with a young family, John stayed in LA while
Michael ran the London salon. The same year, Michaeljohn introduced its own line of products, something of a bold step for any
business other than a multinational haircare company.

In the early 90s, the original London salon moved across the
street. Considerably larger than when it first opened its doors,
Michaeljohn today occupies a unique position at the forefront of
British fashion and style. The success of the satellite salons in and
around London and Beverly Hills has much to do with Michael.

In the 2002 New Year's Honours List Michael was awarded the
Royal Victorian Medal (RVM) - not a political award, but one granted personally by Her Majesty the Queen. Michael thinks of his RVM
as not simply a personal award, but an acknowledgement of the UK
hairdressing industry's considerable achievements and important
contribution to the British economy.

When I met Michael at his flat off Baker Street, he was as always
smart and smiling. Over coffee, he told me about the day he styled
Elizabeth Taylor's hair for a photoshoot. A beautiful pearl, care-
lessly thrown in amongst a dish of hairpins, caught his eye.
Immediately, he recognised it as Le Peregrina, originally owned by
Mary Queen of Scots and given to Elizabeth by Richard Burton.
"That's beautiful. Didn't it belong to Mary Queen of Scots?" he asked.
To which the actress replied: "Nah, it's mine."
Point taken.

TONY AND OZZIE ARE REMARKABLY MODEST ABOUT THE REPUTATION THEY HAVE EARNED IN THEIR 20 YEARS AND MORE AT THE TOP OF HAIRDRESSING.

WHEN THEY FIRST ARRIVED IN ENGLAND FROM ITALY IN THE EARLY 60S, TONY'S HOBBY WAS AMATEUR BOXING. HE MUST HAVE BEEN RATHER GOOD BECAUSE HE WENT ON TO WIN THE JUNIOR ABA TITLE. BY 1973, SEARCHING FOR A MORE CREATIVE PATH IN LIFE, TONY WITH BROTHERS OZZIE AND RICCI, TRAINED AT SASSOON, WHERE HE BECAME INTERNATIONAL ARTISTIC DIRECTOR OVERSEEING EDUCATION IN THE SALONS AND SCHOOLS, AND OZZIE EUROPEAN ART DIRECTOR.

The trio now own the sophisticated Sanrizz salons in prime London locations, and one in Cambridge. The stunning Knightsbridge salon is home to a steady flow of celebrities and is regularly used as a setting for TV programmes. As managing director, Tony divides his time between the Knightsbridge salon, international exhibitions, shows and seminars. In 1998, he opened the highly regarded Hair & Beauty Education Centre near Harrods.

As creative director, Ozzie oversees the activities of the Sanrizz creative team whose philosophy is to reflect style and strength of cutting with a feminine flair. His skills don't stop at hairdressing. Taking most of the photographs on his award-winning Sanrizz shoots, his understanding of photography has earned him considerable praise from British print editors. "There is nothing better than seeing your idea realised in the glossy pages of a magazine," he enthuses. Ozzie's modesty and fondness for his craft make him a popular figure in the industry.

Our paths first crossed in 1982, when Tony founded the world-famous Alternative Hair Show, in memory of his son Valentino who died at the tragic age of two. Almost £5 million has been raised for leukemia research. Every year, star hairdressers from around the world unite for free to let their creative hairs down in this sell-out extravaganza. "I never envisaged that I'd receive such dedication from my fellow hairdressers over so many years, but the continuing success of The Alternative speaks volumes for our industry's big heart. Who would want to work in any other business?" he says.

In September 1999, Tony launched the Alternative Hair Care range. Ten percent of every sale goes towards funding a leukemia research helpline. I have great admiration for all he's achieved and believe his charity deserves to be honoured. Like Ozzie, Tony is one of life's good guys.

Photos: Irvine Rusk

IRIVNE RUSK IS THE BRAVEHEART OF THE BEAUTY INDUSTRY. AT A TIME WHEN THE INDUSTRY WAS DOMINATED BY HAIRDRESSERS FROM LONDON, IRVINE WAS THE OUTSIDER. BUT WITH HIS INIMITABLE SENSE OF STYLE AND OBSESSIVE DETERMINATION, HE WAS THE FIRST TO SHATTER THE MYTH THAT YOU HAD TO BE FROM A MAJOR CITY TO MAKE YOUR MARK. HE BURST DOWN THE DOORS FOR OTHERS TO FOLLOW. BORN IN THE SMALL SCOTTISH TOWN OF BELLSHILL (WHERE YOU SIMPLY DIDN'T BECOME A LADIES' HAIRDRESSER), IRVINE STARTED TRAINING AT 15 WITH JULIUS LIVERANI IN GLASGOW. "FROM THE VERY BEGINNING I WAS IMMERSED IN A WORLD OF BEAUTIFUL HAIRDRESSING," SAYS IRVINE. AT 21 HE LEFT TO START HIS OWN BUSINESS - WITH AN INITIAL STAFF OF SIX THAT EXPANDED INTO A TEAM OF A HUNDRED IN THREE SALONS.

In 1976, Irvine took London by storm in the second ever Salon International, after which he was invited do international show hairdressing. And the world began to learn about Irvine Rusk.

To get more exposure, Irvine started creating whacky hairstyles. In 1984, he revolutionised haircutting with the invention of the weaving blade, which allowed us hairdressers creative freedom in texturising and dimensional cutting. After a couple of years of gimmicks, Irvine's work became much more sophisticated and the respect that followed culminated in 1987 when the ebullient Scot was crowned British Hairdresser of the Year.

By then he set out "to make cool shampoo in cool bottles," and in 1989 he relocated to America where he founded Rusk, once again shaking up the industry with a combination of cutting-edge packaging, innovative ingredients and the consistent launch of new product categories. Supporting him in every step of the way was his wife Louise, whom he first met at his Glasgow salon, a fellow Scot, creative director and inspiration.

In March 2003, Irvine hung up his scissors and Rusk Inc. "After 14 years I'd had enough. I hadn't had a day off since I was 16 years old - it was time to take time out," he explains. That same year he was honoured with a Lifetime Achievement Award at the North American Hairdressing Awards.

Today, Irvine is taking it easy by the ocean at his home in Connecticut, enjoying his children, shooting game and pondering the title of the next chapter in the Remarkable Life of Rusk. "What I decide to do next will probably be a bigger surprise to me than anyone else."

JOHN SANTILLI IS THE MAN WHO TRAINED WITH VIDAL SASSOON FROM THE MID-60S TO 1977, CREATING THE GRADUATED BOB, GREEK GODDESS, THE 5 POINT AND ISADORA HAIRCUTS FOR THE SASSOON ACADEMY. SO ALL YOU LADIES READING THIS, BLAME JOHN FOR ALL THOSE EXCITING HAIRCUTS.

Rising through the Sassoon ranks, he rubbed shoulders with today's most famous hairdressing names, including Trevor Sorbie, Herta Kella and Bruno Mascolo, and by 1973 was director of the new Academy, teaching students how to "cut outside the box." Artistically, this was the most exciting period of John's career. "Full of new ideas about femininity and beauty, I persuaded the company that cutting alone was not good enough - we had to offer colouring courses too. From then on, we used primary colours extensively".

Inspired by Flint Wincopf and Daryl Benson of Burlington's, by 1975 he had taught over 10,000 hairdressers worldwide. This is when John began to earn his nickname, the 'Itinerant Teacher'. His motto could well be "Have scissors, will travel".

"The day in 1977 that I left Sassoon's was a day of reckoning. The door was closed behind me, the future lay ahead," recalls John, whose Italian mother moved to England to marry his father after the war. That year, he began a seven-year world tour, including two years in Japan, where he did shows with Tony Rizzo under the Sanrizz banner, and later opened an English concept salon.

John is the only hairdresser I know who doesn't do hair photography, and works exclusively in Rome where he moved in 1984 to open a school introducing Italians to British styles and cuts. Italy showed their appreciation in 1987 by awarding him the CACF and naming him one of the top three hairdressers in the country.

Today, retired from international exhibitions, John is in a position to achieve what he wants most of all: to give back. "I think everyone in the industry should give time to teach the younger people, especially those who can't afford the best training."

2004: "Time to give back..."
1991: Retires from international exhibitions
1984: Opens hairdressing school in Rome, Italy
       Awarded the CACF
1980: Opens English concept Academy, Japan
1977: Starts a seven-year world tour
1976: Director of the new Sassoon Academy, Knightsbridge
1973: Director of the Vidal Sassoon Academy
1969: Creates Isadora
1966: Moves to Sloane Street salon, under Stephen Way
1964: Joins Vidal Sassoon on Bond Street, under Joshua Galvin

VIDAL'S SUCCESS STORY IS THE MOST REMARKABLE OF ANY HAIRDRESSER'S. IT MERITS ITS OWN BOOK.
HE MAY HAVE TAKEN A BACK SEAT IN THE INDUSTRY FOR THE LAST DECADE, BUT LIKE ALL TRUE TRENDSETTERS, EVERYBODY KNOWS HIS NAME. SASSOON IS HAIRDRESSING.

The 14-year-old lad's mother wanted him to learn a trade. Acting on an ominous dream in which she saw Vidal in a hairdressers' shop, she convinced him to go with her to Cohen's Beauty and Barber Shop in London's East End. Here was an unschooled boy with a thick cockney accent, no experience, and parents who couldn't afford the normal apprentice fee. But Vidal's good manners won the day; Professor Cohen hired him.

For the next six years Vidal swept floors, shampooed customers, always trying to learn more about the business, all the while ridding himself of his unfashionable accent. At night, the teenage Vidal joined his mother in working for Zionist and anti-Fascist organisations. His principles led him to fight in Israel's War of Independence, which ended with the partition of Palestine in 1948. At 20, he was serving in the Palmach, one of the military units that eventually merged to become the Israeli Defense Force. For a year he fought in the Negev Desert campaign.

Back in Britain, Vidal was determined to achieve success in the hairdressing business, his career taking off when backers put up the money for his first salon, a third-floor walk-up on Mayfair's Bond Street so small that customers often had to wait out in the hall. In 1958, he opened his first large Bond Street salon.

All the time he kept searching for new ways to cut hair. "It took nine years of trying to discover ways to make cuts simple, yet elegant, striking to the eye, but somehow natural," says Vidal. "The process involved thinking of hair styling as an extension of someone's total appearance."

With the 60s came a colourful explosion of creative energy from Vidal and many others in Britain. Suddenly, the world seemed better for the new music, styles, ideas and bright young things that the decade brought: the Beatles, Mary Quant, the miniskirt, Carnaby Street, Vidal Sasson's unique cuts. Over the next three

decades the world looked to Vidal for his talent and vision. Fashion designers, Vogue models, movies stars (his $5,000 haircut of Mia Farrow on the set of *Rosemary's Baby* made world headlines) came to him for what was known as Sassooning. The idea of women being able to wash and dry their hair daily, without having to resort to curlers, perms, hairspray or another trip to the hair salon is acceptable now because of Vidal's pioneering efforts. His "wash and wear" hair changed personal style forever.

Vidal's achievements are too numerous to fit on these pages. Whoever said that he changed the way the world looks was right. Over a million hairdressers have trained at his European and North American Academies, and there are now 26 Vidal Sassoon Salons and 13 Vidal Sassoon Schools and Educational Centres worldwide. In 1980, he starred in his own daily TV show.

I remember when he was establishing himself on Bond Street, my wife and I were doing the same in Hampstead. I was writing for the Hampstead & Highate Express, a local weekly newspaper, and Hair & Beauty magazine. Armed with my press pass, Vidal and I would mingle with the great names in the industry at the Paris couture fashion collections. We enjoyed seeing that season's fashion in the making, and then taking them back home and turning them into British looks.

We stayed at the Hotel du Ministère on Rue de Surène - the place to be. It was where all the top London and American models stayed, along with Brian Duffy the great fashion photographer, and Len Deighton who was researching and writing one of his novels. These were such creative and wonderful times.

I arrived early for Vidal's photoshoot for this book and settled down to read the paper by the Carlton Tower hotel poolside, knowing he spends his early mornings keeping fit. After an hour, I began to panic - Vidal is never late. When I eventually got through to his hotel room he answered with: "I left you a message earlier to say I slipped in the rain last night. I slipped, pulling Rhonda (his wife) with me and we both crashed to the floor. I broke two ribs, but do not worry Hesche (his name for me), I can make it this afternoon. Can you reschedule me for 2pm after I've met Vogue?" That's some friend.

Not so many years ago, when I attended Terry Donavan's memorial service on Hanover Square, Princess Diana, Lady Thatcher, Barry Lategan, David Bailey and many other major names from the fashion and beauty world were there. When it was time to leave, I walked with Vidal to the BBC, where his car was parked. Crossing Oxford Street, he turned me and hugged me saying: "Hesche, we've been mates for over 50 years." To me it seems like yesterday.

2003: Regis Corporation buys international Vidal Sassoon Salons & Schools
Sassoon Studio Nottingham opens
2000: The Collection videos launched
1998: Begins sponsorship of New York Fashion Week
1997: Washington, D.C. Salon opens
1996: Miami, Florida Salon and Education Centre opens
1995: Atlanta, Georgia Salon opens
1994: Receives the Degree of Doctor Philosophiae Honoris Causa from the Hebrew University of Jerusalem
Berlin, Germany Salon opens
Begins sponsorship of London Fashion Week
1992-3: 50 Year Retrospective Worldwide Tour
1992: 50 Years Ahead published
1991: 2nd Salon in New York opens
Scottsdale, Arizona Salon opens
1989: Boston, Massachusetts Salon opens
Whiteley's Salon, London opens
1987: Frankfurt, Germany Salon opens
1985: 30 Year Retrospective Exhibition launches at the Hamilton Gallery, London
Procter & Gamble buys Richardson-Vicks
1984: Sassoon appointed Official Hair Stylist to Los Angeles Olympics
1983: Salons/Schools sold to former long time Vidal Sassoon employees. Currently owned by Phillip Rogers and Annie Humphreys
Product Division sold to Richard-Vicks
1980: Corporate offices move to the Century City Twin Towers, Century City, CaliforniaVidal's Your New Day television show started

1978: Continues worldwide media tours including television, health, beauty, hour-long fashion specials
1977: Vidal Sassoon products introduced to mass markets worldwide
1976: Main London School opens
1975: Best selling book, Year of Beauty & Health published
Begins nationwide television guest blitzing to promote book
Opened 130 Sloane Street Salon, London
1974: Corporate offices opens in Century City, California
1973: South Molton Street Salon, England opens
Munich, Germany Salon opens
London Academy opens
Vidal Sassoon original three-step haircare products introduced to trade.
1971: Barber Shop in Bonwit Teller, New York opens
Grant Street Salon in San Francisco, California opens
North Rush Street Salon in Chicago, Illinois opens
1969: Beverly Hills, California Salon opens
First Vidal Sassoon School in the UK
1967: Creates the Greek Goddess, predecessor of today's non-set perm
1965: Opens first USA Salon in New York with Lanvin-Charles of the Ritz
1964: Creates 5-Point Cut which epitomized the Sassoon technique
1963: Creates the classic Bob
1958: Opens first large Bond Street Salon
Creates The Shape - revolutionary cut which founded the Sassoon technique
1954: Opens small third floor walk-up Bond Street Salon, Mayfair
1942: Apprentice to Professor Adolph Cohen
1928: 17th January, born in London

HEINZ'S CAREER BEGAN AGED 14 WHEN HE STARTED CUTTING HAIR AT THE HOLIDAY RESORT OF CARINTHIA IN HIS HOMELAND, AUSTRIA. AS THE SWINGING 60S GATHERED MOMENTUM, HE MOVED TO LONDON WHERE HE WORKED WITH RAYMOND, FRENCH OF LONDON, AND STEINER OF MAYFAIR.

ADHERING TO HIS MOTTO "MAKE THE MOST OF YOUR TALENTS", HEINZ TOOK HIS AROUND THE GLOBE WITH P&O CRUISES, RETURNING IN 1969 TO WORK IN UK DEPARTMENT STORES SUCH AS HARRODS, WHERE HE MET "THE GRANDMASTER", AS HE FLATTERINGLY CALLS ME!

In 1973, Heinz founded Intercrimpers, an educational group of hairdressers, soon followed by his first Schumi salon. Over the next few years, his renowned cutting skills led to 10 new salons, employing over 100 staff throughout fashionable London.

By this time, Heinz with his talented brother, Gregor, was involved editorial work for the UK's top newspapers and glossy magazines. Among the first to advocate wet products not tested on animals, he was also responsible for other innovations, such as the use of herbs in shampoo. The Schumi name hit the headlines again that decade when Heinz devised many of the Punk hairstyles that so symbolised the anti-establishment movement of the time.

Schumi Shapers - those clever, bendy rollers synonymous with the 'big hair' so popular in the 80s - were on all fashion and beauty journalists' 'must have' lists. Later, Heinz became involved in working as a contract filler, producing shampoos for other companies, while his own products continued to sell worldwide.

Among those who have graced Heinz's salon include Diana Ross, Charlotte Rampling, Julie Christie and Marie Helvin. And let's not forget the men - Roger Daltrey, Mick Jagger and Eric Clapton. Celebrities still frequent his latest salon in Chelsea. So what of the future? "I forecast hair being cut off in chunks near the root," says Heinz. "The remaining hair will be coloured to produce a unique look. There will always be a demand for classic cuts - but with a twist: the artistic talents of the hairdresser will be in demand like never before."

This is typical of the way Heinz talks about colour. From the day we first met in Barkers of Kensington, I've found him a most interesting individual. I said as much to my then boss, Arthur Fabricant, MD of Seligman & Latz, describing Heinz as a star in the making and proposing a higher position in a better store. Sadly, Arthur didn't recognise the talent and lost Heinz to Sassoon. The man is a bundle of energy, someone I remain very fond of.

Photo: Angelo Seminara

Photo: Trevor Leighton

HAIRDRESSING HAS BEEN A PASSION FOR ANGELO SEMINARA SINCE CHILDHOOD. CREATIVE AND VISIONARY, HIS PHILOSOPHY IS TO MAKE WOMEN FEEL FEMININE, FASHIONABLE AND PAMPERED.

"I THINK WOMEN ARE VERY INTELLIGENT CREATURES WHOM I RESPECT AND WANT TO MAKE LOOK BEAUTIFUL", HE SAYS.

Trained as a barber in his home town in Italy, he moved to Toni and Guy Salvaggio's salons in Rome before arriving in the UK in 1995 and joining the Trevor Sorbie salon where he's currently creative director. Whilst his forté is cutting edge, high-fashion styles, Angelo will always allow clients to guide him to the cut they desire.

In high demand for show and photographic work, he's been assisting Eugene Soulieman at seminars and designer fashion shows in New York, London, Milan and Paris, where his work has brought him national recognition.

Angelo's ambition is to be among the world's best salon and session hairdressers, and achieving it, retire to a remote island. He has accomplished a great deal for his 32 years, yet his style and talent are still not in full bloom. He is young and vital with a tremendous future to look forward to, creating new images and beautifying a growing base of loyal clients.

2003: Avant Garde Hairdresser of the Year
2002: Avant Garde Hairdresser of the Year Nominee
2000: Avant Garde Hairdresser of the Year
1999: Avant Garde Hairdresser of the Year Nominee
1998: Newcomer of the Year Nominee
1997: Newcomer of the Year Nominee

Photo: Umberto Giannini

AT THE TENDER AGE OF 31, LISA SHEPHERD IS SYNONYMOUS WITH EXPERT COLOURING. YOUNG, PASSIONATE AND AMBITIOUS, SHE IS A STAR IN HER OWN RIGHT. RENOWNED FOR HER OUTSPOKEN, DOWN-TO-EARTH APPROACH, SHE HAS A NATURAL TALENT FOR MAKING EVEN THE WORST HEAD OF HAIR LOOK SENSATIONAL.

In 2002, Lisa returned to the Midlands to launch her first solo venture - Lisa Shepherd Midlands - a forward-looking salon striving to extend the boundaries of the hairdressing world. Designed by Lisa herself, it is a chic, minimalist salon where everyone is encouraged to feel at home. Reflecting her own personality, there's no fuss or formality. The Kidderminster lass has coloured the hair of some of Britain's top names, amongst them popstars S Club 7 and the Sugarbabes. Her most loyal fan is TV's golden girl, Claire Sweeney. She might not be famous, but Annie Gabb is a regular client who once asked Lisa to match her hair colour to a hen - the speckled one sitting mutely in her basket!

Lisa's career began 15 years ago as a colour technician for the late Umberto Giannini, whom she helped find a chain of salons in London and the Midlands, and develop his highly successful product range. "Umberto opened my eyes to the world of hair - the industry, the glamour. The hairdressing he showed me was a career, not a job. He gave me the belief to succeed", she says.

Young and outspoken, Lisa's ambitions are to open more salons across the Midlands and in London, launch a product line, perhaps even a home care and beauty range, become Midlands Hairdresser of the Year for a third time, and win British Colour Technician of the Year. Her ultimate goal is to become British Hairdresser of the Year. Watch this space.

2003: Midlands Hairdresser of the Year
    Winner of Independent Salon Business Newcomer (BHBA)
    Winner of Most Wanted Look
    Schwarzkopf Professional British Colour Technician of the Year

2002: Opened Lisa Shepherd Midlands
1999: Midlands Hairdresser of the Year
1998: Midlands Hairdresser of the Year

ROBERT'S REASON FOR BECOMING A HAIRDRESSER SEEMS TO HAVE BEEN TO MEET GOOD-LOOKING GIRLS. HAIRDRESSING WASN'T IN THE BLOOD - HIS FAMILY WAS IN THE TOY BUSINESS WHEN HE BEGAN SHAMPOOING AT 12-YEARS-OLD.

IN 1967, HE BEGAN TRAINING AT THE LEGENDARY LEONARD SALON IN LONDON, QUALIFYING AS A STYLIST AT THE TENDER AGE OF 18. A MAJOR PART OF HIS EXPERIENCE WAS TO WORK PERSONALLY WITH LEONARD HIMSELF, AT ONE TIME HELPING HIM CREATE HUGE WIGS FOR THE KEN RUSSELL COSTUME DRAMA BARRY LYNDON. "IT WAS A FABULOUS TIME IN HAIRDRESSING," HE RECALLS. "THE PARTIES, THE GLAMOUR, THE PEOPLE, THE PHOTOGRAPHERS - WE WERE SOCIALLY ACCEPTABLE FOR THE FIRST TIME."

He was planning to leave Leonard in July 1973, when he agreed to join friends Neville Tucker and Daniel Hersheson in opening a new salon. "A few months later Leonard found out and fired me. We opened Neville Daniel the following February," he says.

In retrospect, neither he, Neville nor Daniel had much knowledge of running a business: "We were simply busy hairdressers with a loyal clientele and no great competition. We grew organically and made money." Robert enjoyed regular holidays in the Caribbean, acquired a Porsche convertible, a three-bedroomed flat in Hampstead and a beautiful wife. Belinda and he remain happily married 28 years on.

After 14 years in the Neville Daniel partnership, Robert took over their Marylebone salon, re-opening it with new partner Phillip Leighton as the award-winning Shipton & Leighton. Over the next decade, Robert worked with Paul Mitchell and Sebastian, training hairdressers in salon management. In 1999, feeling the need for a sabbatical, he sold the salon to Phillip, with the aim of "travelling the world and doing a bit of gardening."

Relaxed and rested, back amongst beautiful women, Robert is styling and helping structure the management at John Frieda. "I felt his was probably the best salon in London to come to. John and I were juniors at Leonard, and our sons Ben and Jordan went to school together," Robert explains.

He thinks British hairdressing is improving all the time. "I've travelled all over with my job and I've never seen better hairdressing than in the UK," he says.

What does he think of hairdressers as celebrities in their own right? "Good luck to them. But we must remember what we're in the business for: to make stars look and feel good. We are part of a process - not the process itself. Fame is a rub off of the people we work with."

Photo: Anthony Mascolo

Everyone has a kind word to say about Trevor. Anthony Mascolo acknowledges him as "one of the best hairdressers ever, both directionally and creatively." Fellow household name, Charles Worthington, credits him with changing the industry's agenda. Meanwhile, Trevor's hero is Vidal Sassoon.

In spite of legendary status, celebrity clientele, glittering awards, TV appearances and glossy column inches, Trevor remains true to his Scottish roots. "My parents taught me to be a nice person, to respect everyone and always do my best," he explains. It is an indication of how well-known he is that he's been the subject of general knowledge questions on top British TV game shows *Who Wants To Be A Millionaire?* and *The Weakest Link*.

WHAT CAN ONE WRITE ABOUT TREVOR THAT HASN'T BEEN WRITTEN BEFORE? I COULD TRY BY SAYING: HE'S WON MORE AWARDS THAN ANY OTHER, ENJOYS UNIVERSAL RESPECT, AND THE WORLD IS HIS SALON.

The son and grandson of barbers, he left school at 15 with dreams of being a famous artist - an ambition he's arguably achieved. A humorous and charming entertainer, Trevor keeps the audience of his one-man shows spellbound for up to two hours with a blend of cutting, commentary and styling. Artist he may be, but his favourite sound remains that of tills ringing!

A HUMBLE MAN, HE CONTINUES TO EXCITE THE IMAGINATION WITH EVERYTHING HE DOES, MANY OF HIS IDEAS EVENTUALLY SETTING FIRM IN THE HAIRDRESSING CANON. CUTS AND STYLING TECHNIQUES SUCH AS THE WEDGE, THE CHOP AND THE STYLE THAT EVERY WOMAN KNOWS -THE SCRUNCH - ARE ALL TREVOR'S CREATIONS. NO WONDER HE'S WON THE COVETED BRITISH HAIRDRESSER OF THE YEAR TITLE AN UNRIVALLED FOUR TIMES.

"I realise that I'm on the tail-end of my career, but I still have things to do, styles to create, to leave my creative stamp on the world," says Trevor. Despite this self-assurance, his career hasn't all been plain sailing. He admits to over-confidence when starting out. "I spent hours setting and styling an up-do. But as the client walked out it dropped like a stone. That day I decided to learn how to put hair up properly," he says.

I had a wonderful time taking shots of him in his riverside home overlooking Battersea Power station. I really wanted to photograph him enjoying one of his other passions - cooking. But he'd come back on a late flight and hadn't had a chance to shop. Nevermind, spending a few hours with the man was still a joy.

Photo: Al Mc Donald

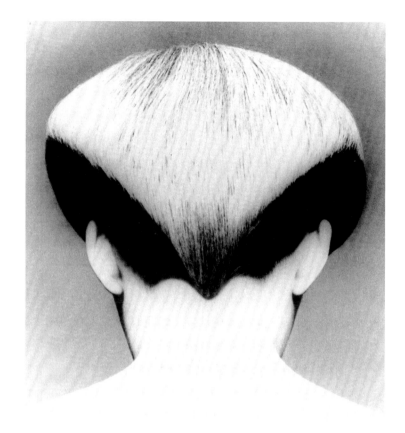

Vogue

2004: Opens salon in Brighton
1999: Opens new salon in Covent Garden
   Launch of Mg - Male grooming product range
   Launch of Style Solutions international product line
1986: Creates the Trevor Sorbie Professional product line
1985: British Hairdresser of the Year
1979: Opens Trevor Sorbie salon, Covent Garden, London
1978: Stylist and session hairdresser at Toni & Guy, then John Frieda

1973: Artistic Director, Vidal Sassoon
1972: Stylist at Vidal Sassoon
1971: Stylist at Selfridges, Ilford
   Stylist at Henri, Loughton
1970: Richard Henry School of Hairdressing
1969: pens a barber shop, Edmonton
1964: Apprentice barber to father, Ilford
1949: Born Paisley, Scotland

Photo: Taggart/Winterhalter

Photo: Anthony Mascolo

AWARDS

2003: AHFA British Master's Award
     First Patron of Honour for the Fellowship of Australian
     Hairdressing
2002: Pantene Pro V Celebrity Hairdresser of the Year
     Aveda Master of the Arts
2001: Grand Trophy of the Professional Press, AIPP
1999: Best Celebrity Hairdresser, Pantene Pro-V Awards
     Awarded Fellowship of the City and Guilds of London
     Institute (FCGI)
1997: Best Haircutter Worldwide
     Most Newsworthy Male Worldwide (IBS Award)
1996: Most Newsworthy Male Worldwide (IBS Award)
     Finalist British Hairdresser of the Year

1995: World Congress Hall of Fame
     Living Legend Award New York
     Finalist British Hairdresser of the Year
1993: Patron D'Honneur Lifetime Hairdressing Award
     Best Education Award (USA)
1992: British Hairdresser of the Year
1991: British Hairdressing Hall of Fame
     British Hairdresser of the Year
Avant Garde Stylist of the Year
1990: Foreign Stylist of the Year, Peluquerias magazine
1989: London Stylist of the Year
1986: British Hairdresser of the Year
     London Stylist of the Year
1985: British Hairdresser of the Year
     National Hairdresser of the Year
     Joint London Hairdresser of the Year

Photos: Paolo Roversi

SOMETHING OF A TRUE VISIONARY, EUGENE IS ONE OF TODAY'S MOST INFLUENTIAL HAIR STYLISTS, WHOSE HUMOUR AND UNIQUE WAY OF LOOKING AT HAIR PERMEATES HIS AVANT-GARDE STYLE. AS HIS HAIR SCULPTURES TESTIFY, HE STRIVES TO PUSH ACCEPTED BOUNDARIES, TAKING RISKS WITH BOTH COLOUR AND LENGTH.

BUBBLY AND CREATIVE, HIS SMILE AND FLARE FOR NEW LOOKS TAKE HIM AROUND THE WORLD, WORKING WITH BEAUTIFUL WOMEN FROM STAGE, SCREEN AND CATWALK. "PEOPLE SHOULD HAVE FUN WITH HAIR AND NOT BE AFRAID TO TAKE RISKS. AFTER ALL, IF THEY DON'T LIKE THE END RESULT, IT WILL ALWAYS GROW OUT," HE SAYS.

His career began by chance. In 1982, a job centre apprenticed him to a hairdresser. Eugene had found his niche and from that point there was no turning back. For ten years he worked closely with Trevor Sorbie, learning the "Sassoon way", before branching out to create cutting edge trends in his own inimitable style. In 1998 he worked at Toni & Guy, followed by a stint as co-creative director for Bumble and Bumble before being approached by Vidal Sassoon to become their editorial director.

Based in London, he is a regular contributor to top fashion magazines including US Vogue, ID, The Face, Dazed and Confused and the New York Times. His talent for interpreting designers' ideas into hairstyles that complement the clothes means he's constantly in demand for shows such as Chloe, Prada and Hussein Chalayan, with whom he's forged a particularly close relationship.

I had wanted to meet Eugene for a long time when I joined him and his new wife at their Hampstead home in 2003. I still hadn't decided how to photograph him; taking portraits of so many icons is like cutting the hair of 65 friends into different looks - not an easy task. That was until he took me into his magic room of fur, feathers, rollers, wigs, tongs, spray cans, wax… It was like walking into an Aladdin's cave of possibilities. This is where he works out his ideas. I almost felt like checking if it had a red light above the door and a 'Do Not Disturb' sign.

"Doing a haircut is like a jigsaw puzzle," explains Eugene. "You've got all the pieces to put together, and if put together the right way you achieve something beautiful." You have to have been born creative to go this far in the world. Still a young 42, Eugene will continue to surprise art directors with what's up his sleeve.

I FOUND LEE AT HIS NEW FLAT OVERLOOKING THE STATUE OF EROS ON PICCADILLY CIRCUS, A FAR CRY FROM HIS HOME AND THE LOCATION OF HIS FIRST SALON - THE HOUSE THAT HAIR BUILT - IN LEIGH-ON-SEA. FROM A LARGE FAMILY AND NOT SHORT OF FRIENDS, THE ESSEX BOY HAD PLENTY OF OPPORTUNITY TO PRACTISE WHEN HE STARTED CUTTING HAIR AS A TEENAGER IN HIS MUM'S LIVING ROOM.

"I JUST PICKED UP A PAIR OF SCISSORS AND CUT STREET HAIRSTYLES - SHORT BACK AND SIDES AND A QUIFF ON TOP WAS THE FASHION", HE SAYS. "WHEN I WENT ON TO HAIRDRESSING SCHOOLS IN LONDON I WAS INITIALLY OVERWHELMED; I THOUGHT I'D BITTEN OFF MORE THAN I COULD CHEW".

Eight years, on he's won Men's British Hairdresser of the Year, become a household name through television (Essex Wives, This Morning, The Salon...) and has his own problem-solving product line - Lee Stafford Haircare - sold worldwide, most recently in Australia. With Schiaparelli pink packaging and names such as 'the double blow' and 'as rough as you like', the range has Lee's out-there signature all over it. Young, fun celebrities such as Dido and Leah Wood find his playful personality refreshing and exciting.

"I'm like a sponge - I want to keep moving upwards and onwards. I don't want to be top of the charts and then fade like so many modern celebrities. I love my new flat, my salons, my staff, and I want to make my success bigger and better," says the 37-year-old in his jeans, vest, and tattoos.

I learnt a lot in my five hours with Lee - How to Make It, if I had my time all over again. A rough diamond, this is just the beginning for the bad boy.

STEINER'S STORY BEGAN IN 1926, WHEN HE LEFT SCHOOL TO JOIN THE LONDON FAMILY SALON, ON THE DEATH OF HIS FATHER. IN JUST OVER A DECADE, HE WENT ON TO OPEN HIS OWN IN MAYFAIR, SELLING HIS OWN RANGE OF HAIR AND PERSONAL CARE PRODUCTS, AND PIONEERING THE BEAUTY PRODUCT INDUSTRY AS WE KNOW IT TODAY.

IN 1947 STEINER WAS GRANTED THE HONOUR OF BEING APPOINTED HAIRDRESSER TO QUEEN MARY, (FOLLOWED IN 1970, BY APPOINTMENT AS COSMETICIANS TO HER MAJESTY THE QUEEN MOTHER). BY 1956, STEINER SALONS WERE ESTABLISHED THROUGHOUT ENGLAND, AND THE COMPANY WON ITS FIRST CONTRACT ON BOARD THE CRUISE SHIP ANDES, FOLLOWED SHORTLY BY THE QUEEN ELIZABETH AND SEVERAL OTHER LUXURY TRANSATLANTIC LINERS. FEW CRUISE PASSENGERS WILL NOT HAVE STROLLED PAST A STEINER HAIR & BEAUTY SALON. WHAT FORESIGHT.

Shrewd and forward-thinking, and recognising the subtle changes in women's attitudes towards beauty, Steiner became, in the 60s, the first British hairdresser to introduce massage and facials onto his menu of services. He was musical, artistic, and a keen collector of art and antiques. Before joining the family business, he dreamt of becoming a great violinist. The clothes worn by the dolls you see in the picture were crafted by his hands.

Steiner's daughter, Michele Warshaw, once kindly showed me around his beautiful Hampstead home with its collection of 18th century Spanish combs, and a lock of Napoleon's hair. As it happens, I hadn't long photographed fellow-hairdresser Eugene Soulieman who owns a valuable set of Japanese dolls. I found it interesting that both should be collectors.

I had the pleasure of meeting Steiner many years ago at a dinner party. Although I was aware of his history on the cruise liners, I never saw him at hair shows, or at the Fellowship. Unlike Raymond or Freddy French, he kept himself to himself.

By 1994, the Steiner maritime business had grown to boast 54 salons, including on board the QE2, the first ship spa to feature a thalassotherapy pool and inhalation chambers. At one time, allowed only a small area in the depth of the ship, the new salons now took over prime space on the top decks.

Not long after, the company sold all the salons in England and acquired Elemis, a luxury lifestyle range of premium plant-based products. Today Steiner Leisure is the largest spa provider in the world. "I don't think my father would have been surprised at our success," says Michele. "He always said that one day the beauty business would be bigger for us than hairdressing."

RAYMOND'S IS A CLASSIC RAGS-TO-RICHES STORY.
BORN TO AN IMMIGRANT ITALIAN BARBER AND HIS FRENCH WIFE,
HE GREW UP A CHEEKY TRILINGUAL BOY IN SOHO, WHERE HOME
WAS THE BASEMENT OF THE BARBER SHOP. IN CONTRAST, AT
THE HEIGHT OF HIS FAME HE OWNED HOUSES IN THE ENGLISH
COUNTRYSIDE, KNIGHTSBRIDGE AND THE SOUTH OF FRANCE.

FLAMBOYANT AND FEARLESS,
RAYMOND ACHIEVED A STRING OF HAIRDRESSING FIRSTS.

At just 20 years old, five years after joining, he became the youngest teacher at the Societe de Progrès de la Coiffure and was appointed superintendent the following year. His original Mayfair salon, opened 1936, was remarkable for its innovative open-plan, cubicle-free design. And what a sumptuous salon it was: its crystal chandeliers, gold leaf moulded mirrors and Regency chairs epitomised luxury. At the end of the decade, he had the honour of being requested to create the wigs of Vivien Leigh in the all-time classic film, *Gone With the Wind*, on the set of which his famous moustache, striking good looks and dapper dress sense frequently got him mistaken for Clark Gable. (Talking of Hollywood, at the end of the 50s, he was offered an unprecedented £3,123 to tend to Diana Dors' hair.)

In 1953, the BBC gave the telegenic Raymond his own weekly TV programme, on which he had the habit of saying "We put a teasie-weasie here, a teasie-weasie there" - hence the rise of his international nickname, Teasie Weasie. The little side kiss curls became a trend overnight. He inherited a love of horses and gambling from his mother, and was the first hairdresser to own two Grand National winners; Ayala in 1963 and Rag Trade in 1976. An unconventional leader of hair fashion for half a century, at their height, his chain of salons employed over a thousand staff and cared for more than 10,000 clients a week. "My aim has always been to make beautiful women even more beautiful, and to bring out the beauty of plain women by adding that little bit that God seems to have overlooked," he once said.

I had the thrill of meeting God (as we sometimes called him) on several occasions, perhaps most memorably in the 1950s when he had two salons near Dumas, where I was working at the time. You always knew he was coming because he would sound the horn of his convertible black Cadillac, which mechanically declared "Raymond is here!" The master of publicity, he was not a shy man. At his home on April 17th 1992, aged 80, Raymond lost his courageous 20-year battle with cancer. A legend in his own lifetime, we will always remember him.

1992: Passed away April 17th
1983: Awarded the OBE
1978: Presented with an Oscar by Intercoiffure National Congress
1974: Awarded the Commendatore (equivalent of a Knighthood)
       by the Italians
1965: Married actress Rosalie Ashley
1962: Toured America with his own hair show
1956: Dressed Diana Dors' hair
1953: Five-year contract to appear weekly on BBC TV
1939: Did Vivien Leigh's hair on Gone With the Wind
1936: Opened salon in Mayfair
1933: President, French Academy of Hairdressing and Wig Craft
1929: Grand Prix for Permanent Waves, Paris
1911: Born in London

DURING THE 70S, RICHARD WORKED AT A TOP MANCHESTER SALON, BEFORE THE DECADE CLOSED, CO-FOUNDING MAHOGANY HAIRDRESSING IN OXFORD - AN ENTERPRISE WHICH RAPIDLY GREW INTO A FOUR SALON GROUP.

In the early 90s, he moved back to London to open the flagship Mahogany salon in Mayfair, where he is both managing director and International creative director. "Hair fashion is extremely transient and we continually create styles to meet our clients changing needs. We strive to bridge the gap between the avant-garde and the wearable styles," he says.

2004 sees Richard become president of the Fellowship for British Hairdressing, and part of the British and Austrian Hair Congresses, the Australian Hair Congress and the Palm Springs/LA Shows. He has performed sell-out shows at the British Hair Congress, The British Hair Collections and seminars for Wella in Europe.

Richard's trademark cut is short, sexy, and technically precise - Erin O'Connor's hair is a good example. "I think she is the most enigmatic beauty of our time", says Richard. It's no coincidence that model agencies entrust their new faces to him for that definitive look.

Despite all his commitments, Richard still finds time to tend to a loyal clientele, twice a week in London and one day a week in Oxford. Some clients regularly travel from as far as South Africa, Switzerland, San Diego and (it's true!) Russia.
"A client with long hair came in to me with a picture of a short cut; we agreed it would be fabulous," he recalls.
"As I cut the first section at the ear, the lady fainted. Two thoughts sprang to mind: the first was 'Oh my God!', followed by 'Please come round or I'll be behind.' That was 15 years ago and she's still a client, currently with a short graduation bob and a stronger constitution."

2004: President, Fellowship for British Hairdressing
2002: Vice President, Fellowship for British Hairdressing
2001: Fellowship Hairdresser of the Year
2000: AIPP Avant Garde Hairdresser of the Year

IN HIS BOOK "A YEAR OF BEAUTY AND HEALTH," VIDAL CALLS ROGER "THE BEST CREATIVE CUTTER OF THEM ALL."

Roger joined Vidal Sassoon in 1961, at the Bond Street salon, later being promoted manager of the Grosvenor House salon, which promptly became known as Roger of Vidal Sassoon Grosvenor House. During a year-long American training trip, he took a shine to the country and moved there permanently with his family in 1970.

Three years later, he opened his own salon on New York's 55th Street, where he enjoyed the unusual position of being able to pick and choose those he worked his magic on. Before a single hair was touched, each client was given an extensive consultation. Those who insisted on styles that were wrong for them, or didn't have hair that he could work on charmingly discouraged from returning.

When Vidal set out on his own he would take an hour or more to cut a head of hair, longer if it was complicated. His book Sorry I Kept You Waiting was a direct reference to a typical appointment at his salon; you might be there for hours. This rubbed off on the star staff such as Roger. Many clients were lost, but many more were willing to wait for the adventure.

Fast forward to 1987, when Roger was approached to open a salon at Barney's, the exclusive New York department store, and later a second in their Dallas, Texas store. He worked for both until Barney's went bankrupt. Undeterred, he set up another studio of his own on Madison Avenue. An accumulation of the former international artistic director of Vidal Sassoon's creative experiences and artistic knowledge, he called it the "perfect space to work."

Both Scorpios, Roger and I had hit it off from the moment he joined the Glemby International team on London's Grosvenor Street, where he'd been invited to upgrade the company's cutting techniques. Watching his magical hands at work was like witnessing a force of nature. One of the best hairdressers in the world, he was also a superb sculptor.

In January 1999, Roger was diagnosed with brain cancer. The hardest part of the illness for him was being unable work; cutting hair was how he expressed himself. After a seven-month struggle, he passed away in the presence of his children and loving wife, Shirley.

"I have known Roger for 40 years; he was very special to me. He developed two major breakthroughs way before anyone else. He was the best pair of hands in the business." VIDAL SASSOON

"The man was an artist. Vidal himself said there will never be the likes of Roger again, and he's right." JOSHUA GALVIN

"I feel very privileged to have worked with Roger. His innovative inspiration opened many avenues for today's generation of hairdressers and will continue to do so for years to come." JO HANSFORD

"He was perhaps one of the greatest haircutters I have ever seen." STEPHEN WAY

"His work, whether with clients, magazines, or shows, was always immaculate. Roger cut hair with a feeling and commitment that I have never seen anyone do before. Hairdressers owe a great debt to him." STEPHEN MESSIAS

"Roger's presence and exceptional talent were a joy to watch, and a wonder to work with. He was my valued colleague for many years." ANNIE HUMPHREYS

"Roger had a naturally keen eye for shape and form that made his work impossible to ignore. My admiration for him remains undiminished." TIM HARTLEY

ONCE A HUMBLE FAMILY BUSINESS,
THE TONI & GUY HAIRDRESSING EMPIRE PRESIDED OVER
BY THE FOUR MASCOLO BROTHERS: ANTHONY, BRUNO,
GUY AND TONI, IS TODAY AN INTERNATIONAL NETWORK
OF 400 UPMARKET SALONS.

Their story starts in the 1950s when their hairdresser father, Francesco, his wife Maria, and their four sons emigrated from Pompeii in Italy to London where, soon afterwards, their youngest Anthony was born. Having taught his two eldest boys, Toni (Guiseppe) and Guy (Gaetano) the family trade, in 1963 the father and two sons opened a family business in Clapham, South London - the first Toni & Guy salon. Bruno joined them not long after and the partnership went on to open a further three salons. By the 1970s, having sold three of its businesses, the company had opened a new flagship salon in Mayfair, and was regularly getting work published in magazines. "By this time, Anthony had joined us and we all fell into our natural roles. He was very good creatively; Guy had a talent for photography; Bruno was a natural PR man, and I had a flair for managing people," says Toni. In 1985, Bruno spearheaded their breakthrough into the American market with the opening of the first US Toni & Guy salon in Dallas, Texas. The same year saw the TiGi product range launched, and back in the UK, Anthony won his first British hairdressing award - London Hairdresser of the Year.

Now in its 41st year, the company continues to be run and owned by the four brothers - youngest Anthony, 46. Families can be minefields at the best of times, but throw a multimillion-pound business in the mix and life can get interesting.

I go back a long way with them, from the time when the four young men came to Mayfair with no big reputation, or PR, but with a great deal of conviction and talent. Tough is an understatement, but they won through to direct one of the most successful hairdressing groups in the world.

On Saturday May 24th 2003 I finally photographed the four brothers - a first in this way I was told. What else can I say except that they are a tonic to be with, and I have a great admiration for each of them. Francesco and Maria would have been thrilled that Anthony, Bruno, Tony and Guy remain firm friends and business partners, united in the family name.

ANTHONY MASCOLO IS THE YOUNGEST OF THE FOUR
BROTHERS WHO BUILT THE INTERNATIONAL TONI & GUY
SALON EMPIRE.
HE REMEMBERS BEING A JUNIOR TO HIS LATE FATHER,
FRANCESCO, STANDING ON A BOX TO REACH THE BASIN IN
ORDER TO SHAMPOO CLIENTS' HAIR. INSPIRED BY HIS OLDER
BROTHER BRUNO, IN HIS LATE TEENS ANTHONY WAS WORKING
AS A SESSION HAIRDRESSER WITH MAJOR FASHION AND
BEAUTY PHOTOGRAPHERS THROUGHOUT THE WORLD.

As the family business expanded, Anthony began to concentrate on promotion and education. He is responsible for the phenomenally successful image of Toni & Guy, TIGI, and the more recently introduced Bed Head product range. With the stress he places on motivation in training, he can claim to have revolutionised hairdressing education.

However, Anthony's talents go further than hairdressing. In the 1980s, frustrated by the results of collaborations with photographers, he began taking his own photos, and is now highly respected as a photographer in his own right.

An inspiration to the thousands of Toni & Guy hairdressing staff all over the world, he is admired not only for his creative talent, but for his character and personality. He is always smiling and to this day, I have never seen him in a bad mood. "Enjoy your journey... don't worry about the destination," he advises. As testimony to the truth of his philosophy, Anthony has three times been voted British Hairdresser of the Year, and as head of the UK Toni & Guy Art art team, he has won Best British Art Team a staggering nine times.

Since the Mascolo empire was divided between the brothers in 2002, Anthony has focused on strengthening TIGI and Bed Head haircare worldwide, the latter is currently the No.3 salon brand in America. As creative director he sets trends, each year creating a collection of cuts, colour techniques and styles, which will be the coming season's key looks. These are then taught to all Toni & Guy hairdressers around the world, with the intention of distinguishing the salons from the rest of the throng.

Often shunning media attention, Anthony is at heart a family man and a surprisingly private. Married with three children, he enjoys the support of his wife Pat in his photography and his educational videos, CDs and books. Animated and modest, within hairdressing Anthony remains the perfect figurehead for Toni & Guy.

Photo: Serge Krouglikoff

1978

Photo: Serge Krouglikoff

1979

Photo: Pete Underwood

1985

Photo: Anthony Mascolo

1986

Photo: Antthony Mascolo

1992

Photo: Anthony Mascolo

1993

Photo: Anthony Mascolo

1994

Photo: Anthony Mascolo

1998

NEVILLE WAS FIRST INTRODUCED INTO THE INDUSTRY AS A TEENAGER BY A RELATIVE, HIS UNCLE RICO, OWNER OF A HAIRDRESSING EQUIPMENT BUSINESS, WHO GOT HIM A JOB IN A BUZZY 50-STAFF SALON - THE DELIGHTFULLY TITLED RICHARD CONWAY GINGER GROUP.

"BORN AND BRED IN THE GREY LONDON SUBURB OF EDGWARE, I SUDDENLY FOUND MYSELF IN A GLAMOUROUS NEW WORLD," RECALLS NEVILLE.

Neville pursued his training and qualified as a stylist with the typically elegant London branch of Alexander of Paris, in Bruton Street, before moving on at 19 for a stint with the Robert Fielding salons, managed by Eric Fielding. "I learnt most of what I know about running a successful salon from my grocer father, Bernard, and Eric - two of the best businessmen I know," says Neville.

After a spell styling at Hugos in St John's Wood, Neville excitedly opened a salon with Daniel Hersheson in 1973: "The first day of Neville Daniel was so exhilarating. We were on cloud nine for weeks!" Within three years, the salon had doubled in size. And how times have changed - they charged £2 for a manicure, £5 for a cut.

They went on to acquire a three-storey site on Sloane Street, now occupied by Dolce & Gabbana, followed by a 5,000 square foot salon opposite Harrods, and three years later another on the King's Road. For a decade, Neville Daniel were hairdressers by appointment to her Majesty the Queen.

All good things come to an end. After a long successful partnership Neville and Daniel went their separate ways, leaving the charismatic Neville free to find his glamorous Belgravia salon, Neville Hair and Beauty. With its diverse friendly staff of 40, including colourists and nail technicians, the salon has a reputation for excellence, appealing to a cross-section of society, from locals to jet-setters to royalty.

"Two things are vital to our continued success," says Neville. "For all the glamour you might attach to our location, or who our clients are, my salon is a welcoming place in which the team's rapport makes for a lively, special atmosphere - a necessary step in achieving the second prerequisite: great work. A talent for balancing these beautifully is what gives our clients our signature look of young sophistication."

IN MY ESTIMATION, RICHARDS IS THE NEXT MAN TO LEAD LONDON AS THE EPICENTRE OF HAIR FASHION. DON'T GET ME WRONG, HE'S ALREADY WELL ON THE WAY, BUT ACHIEVING SUPERSTARDOM TAKES TIME, HARD WORK, SUPPORT OF THE PRESS, AND LUCK. WITH A MUCH LARGER, STATE-OF-THE-ART SALON PENDING IN ONE OF LONDON'S MOST PRESTIGIOUS AFTER LOCATIONS, AN INSPIRATIONAL, MOTIVATED TEAM SUPPORTING HIM, AND AN EXCEPTIONAL QUALITY OF CREATIVITY, HE CAN'T FAIL.

He himself acknowledges that opening a salon is the easy part. What comes immediately afterwards is the real eye-opener! "It was so nerve-racking. For a while, my life revolved around how we were going to pay our staff and keep moving forward. But it made me understand that bums on seats really is the most important thing about running a hairdressing business, and that paying staff is the number one priority", recalls Richard.

By the time he took on the Sloane Street salon, in 1992, things were already running fairly smoothly. Renamed Richard Ward Hair & Beauty in 1997, its 55 highly-skilled staff offer more than 100 hair and beauty treatments, spread over two floors. Two in-house chefs and a specialist Tao masseur to cater for clients' other physical requirements!

Richard's unpretentious brand of couture hairdressing has led him, in the words of the Daily Telegraph, to corner the market in young, high profile and celebrity clients. There's no greater draw for new and existing clients than knowing they could be sitting next to Will Young or Tara Palmer-Tomkinson.

"Style-wise, the diffusion of retro and contemporary will mean that hair becomes even more individual and uncontrived. Seasonal impacts may be more transient, while fashion will continue to be a very personal statement - women will feel increasingly comfortable with what suits them, and less pressurised into wearing catwalk looks", forecasts Richard.

"We are lucky that British hairdressing is revered throughout the world - and it seems to be getting better and better. Local salons will continue to improve both their technical ability and choice of services, making a visit part of every woman's budget", he adds.

In Richard's pipeline there's a product range, a BBC documentary, and possibly even a British Hairdresser of the Year Award? He's hungry and he'll make it - *mark my words.*

2001: British Hairdresser of the Year nominee
2000: Joined the Fellowship for British Hairdressing
1999: British Hairdresser of the Year nominee
1992: Bought Neville Daniel
1990 -1992: Hari's, Brompton Cross, senior stylist
1984 - 1990: Neville Daniel, Sloane Street, London - apprentice,
              junior stylist, stylist, senior stylist
1983 - 1984: Daniel Galvin apprentice

STEPHEN WAY'S RAPPORT WITH HAIRDRESSING WAS IMMEDIATE. ATTRACTED TO THE FREEDOM, FUN AND ARTISTRY, HE GOES SO FAR AS TO INSIST THAT ANYONE THINKING OF ENTERING THE PROFESSION MUST FIRST BE "IN LOVE WITH HAIRDRESSING".

Whenever I used to visit Vidal Sassoon at his salons at 108 New Bond Street and then 171 Bond Street in the 50s, Stephen was always around, developing his natural talent. He recalls the time when the postman arrived one morning and loudly announced that he had a letter for Victor Baboon. "You can imagine the look on everyone's faces!" he says.

Stephen has been an aggressive hairdresser (you need aggression to cope with all the travel) working around the world, first for Saks on Fifth Avenue in New York, then the celebrated Carita sisters in Paris, providing a perfect foundation for returning to England to open his own salon on Bond Street.

His working and teaching style have been admired and respected since he first started out. He is one of the characters in the industry that grows on you. His client-base of stars is endless, as is his terrific photographic work. Today, Stephen channels his energy into the presidency of 3-6-5 Day Hairdressing, an organisation dedicated to teaching salon professionals. He believes unshared knowledge inhibits creativity; that we only progress by sharing ideas. A great listener, he has an intuitive understanding of human nature, encouraging people to recognise their strengths and overcome their weaknesses.

One year, John Paul Mitchell Systems sponsored the first night of a re-opening of the musical hit Hair - I always planned a PR event for John Paul Dejoria around his trips to London. For the promotional photoshoot I brought in Sam McKnight as session hairdresser, Stephen as photographer, with the cast of the show as models. The final ingredient of the pre-show event was the celebrities, so we invited rock 'n' roller Roger Daltrey along with my client and TV presenter Gloria Hunniford. I wanted her to be collected rather than have her travel alone in a taxi, so I asked Stephen, who was passing near her home, if he would oblige.

It was a perfect night, no more so than for Stephen and Gloria who are now happily married.

MAXINE AND I LOVE LONG WEEKENDS DOWN ON THE SOUTH-EAST COAST OF ENGLAND, WITH OUR FAVOURITE FRIENDS, X (AS WE CALL HIM) AND HIS BEAUTIFUL WIFE SHERRY. HE SPEAKS SO ELOQUENTLY AND WITH SUCH AN UNDERSTANDING OF THE INDUSTRY THAT I LEARN SOMETHING NEW EVERY TIME WE MEET.

XAVIER WAS A TALENTED AMBASSADOR FOR BRITISH HAIRDRESSING. HE TRAVELLED LIKE A PRINCE WHENEVER HE WAS JUDGING CONTESTS, OR ATTENDING MAJOR INDUSTRY BOARD MEETINGS: HE'D BE IN JAPAN ONE WEEK, PARIS ANOTHER, SOUTH AFRICA THE NEXT.

Born in 1915 in Hoxton, east London, Xavier was the son of a Polish family of hairdressers. From the age of 11, he worked in his father's barbershop, until at 15, he became far more interested in girls than hairdressing. However, just two years later, following his father's death, Xavier took over the responsibility of the family salon.

In 1935, he joined Raymond at his new salon in Grafton Street, Mayfair. The salon made its debut in the heady society days when Mayfair was an exclusive square mile occupied by London's richest socialites. Then war came, interrupting many a promising career, including Xavier's who enlisted as a private and emerged six years later as a major with an MBE for gallantry.

Picking up where he left off, Xavier became a salon manager on London's bustling Regent Street. The following year, he became a founder member of the Fellowship for British Hairdressing where he was president from 1956 to 1958, and subsequently chairman from 1979 to 1990. With his endless enthusiasm and energy, he put the organisation on its present path to prosperity. He also made his name known and respected throughout the hairdressing world as president general of the Paris-based Organisation Artistique Internationale.

Xavier opened his own salon in Knightsbridge in 1952 and remained a well-respected name until he retired in 1979. He recalls one day Eartha Kitt coming in carrying a small Chow dog, which Xavier leant down to stroke. Far from welcoming the attention, it bit him! "Don't worry, Eartha, I was in the war. I've seen blood before," he laughed as he left to have a tetanus injection. Other stars that have had their hair shaped by Xavier's hands include Ronnie Barker, Glenda Jackson, Jeremy Irons, Diane Celento, Leslie Carron, Jenny Agutter, Amy Johnsson and Marlene Dietrich.

Today, in his 80s, Xavier likes to spend his days reading and admiring his Birchington garden, which looks as good as his haircuts.

TWICE BRITISH HAIRDRESSER OF THE YEAR, AND OWNER OF FIVE PRESTIGIOUS LONDON SALONS, CHARLES WORTHINGTON IS UNIVERSALLY ACKNOWLEDGED AS ONE OF THE MOST INFLUENTIAL HAIRDRESSERS ALIVE. A CELEBRITY IN HIS OWN RIGHT, CHARLES CAN BE SUMMED UP IN TWO WORDS: STYLE AND SUCCESS.

He started hairdressing as a teenager washing hair in a York salon, before moving to London at 21 to work with Robert Fielding. By his late 20s Charles has moved to the celebrity world of Betty Jackson fashion shows, but never gave up his vision of making designer haircare accessible to all.

The international launch of his first signature haircare range - Results, in 1986 - coincided with the opening of his first salon in London. The coming decade saw him win a succession of accolades for his innovative cutting and styling - London Hairdresser of the Year, British Hairdresser of the Year and Men's Hairdresser of the Year.

Charles is undoubtedly a leading light in the beauty arena - his growing portfolio of award-winning ranges, including Takeaways, Big Hair, In Fashion brushes and Charles Worthington Electricals, selling worldwide.

Charles' vision is, today, an international reality. In 1999, he unveiled both the flagship salon at No. 7 Percy Street and his groundbreaking Dream Hair range, the first to bring skincare technology to haircare.

One of the keys to his success is his broad appeal and ability to keep ahead of fashion and consumer trends. Charles has tended to the tresses of leading names in film, music and modelling, amongst them Sophie Dahl, Jodie Kidd and Shannon Elizabeth, and can guarantee Hollywood glamour at the Golden Globes and the Oscars. His creativity is given equally free rein at London Fashion Week, when the results of his collaborations with the capital's leading designers regularly make headlines.

2003: Opens first international salon in New York
2000: Flagship salon and spa opens on Percy Street
1989: The Broadgate Club and Covent Garden salons open
1998: British Hairdresser of the Year
        Charles Worthington products launched in America
1997: Charles Worthington Regent's Place opens
1996: British Hairdresser of the Year
1995: Opens salon at the Dorchester Hotel
        Results launched
1986: Opens first salon in Charlotte Place, London

These days, Charles divides his time between the UK and America, where the 2003 opening of the first international Worthington salon prompted Harpers Bazaar to comment: "Charles is a genius... we marvel at his extraordinary, wide-range of trustworthy products. He is a most welcome addition to the New York beauty scene."

What does Charles say? "The salon has been a fantastic success so far; clients have been flooding in since we first opened our doors. The British staff and food are proving very popular, as are the high levels of service we insist upon. Because many of the salons in America have an 'express' feel, the luxury of ours very much appeals to those looking to be pampered."

To follow the likes of Vidal Sassoon and John Frieda in taking on the American challenge in the present circumstances shows real courage.

© 2004 Seven Publications
3, Square Moncey, 75009 Paris, France
T. +33 1 48 74 10 17
info@sevenpublications
www.tribu-te.com

© for the hairdressers photos: Harold Leighton
Texts : Marged Maggie Richards, London
Design: Mathias Dautriat, Paris

Printed in Italy
ISBN 2-9521628-0-8